How to be Radically Free

May this book find itself in the hands of those who are dedicated to their own path of full soul integration, enlightenment, awakening and radical freedom. I dedicate this book to you.

How to be Radically Free

A Handbook for Spiritual Empowerment and Freedom

Louisa Love

ENLIGHTEN
YOURSELF

Disclaimer: Although the author and publisher have made every effort to ensure that the information in this book was correct at press times, the author, publisher and any sub-parties do not assume and hereby disclaim any liability to any party for any loss, damage, or disruption caused by errors or omissions, whether such errors or omissions result from negligence, accidents, or any other cause. This book is not intended as a substitute for the medical advice of physicians. The reader should consult a physician in matters relating to his/her health, and particularly with respect to any symptoms that may require medical attention. The reader accepts all risk. The author does not guarantee you will be healthy or disease-free from reading this work or from trying any suggestions herein. The author is not responsible for external websites mentioned or their content.

Cover Design: Tim Moore
Illustrations: Mary McQuillan

ISBN – 13: 978-1721111107
ISBN – 10: 1721111107

1st Edition, July 2018

ACKNOWLEDGEMENTS

Firstly, I'd like to thank my editor, Jenny, for not only being an awesome support, but also doing all of the editing and formatting for the book. I am deeply grateful for the magic of divine synchronicity that brought you into my life at just the right time so that this book could be birthed. Thank you also to Chris who assisted with the diagrams.

Thank you to my two sons Phoenix and Xavier for keeping me grounded and showing me that I don't need to take life too seriously. I love playing with you! You both inspire me to heal, grow and evolve. Knowing you are here motivates me to write and speak my truth. I love you unconditionally.

I want to thank my friends, my selenite sisters (you know who you are) and my community here in Somerset. I would like to also give a special thanks to my dance community called Everything is Connected here in Frome for allowing me to just be me, shadow and all.

Thank you Alison Manos for helping me heal all those years ago, and for inspiring me to become a Kinesiologist.

Thank you beautiful and expansive Universe for divine synchronicity, magic and for this life journey. Thank you to all parts of myself for ploughing on regardless of immense past pain and suffering, and for committing myself to this incredible path of Radical Freedom!

CONTENTS

Introduction   1

Spiritual Terminologies and Concepts   8

Part I   Purifying the Bodies   25

Part II Mental and Emotional Self Help Healing Tools   29

Part III Clearing Out and Purifying your Physical Body   71

Part IV Healing the Mental and Emotional Bodies   111

Part V Clearing Out and Purifying your Spiritual Body   227

Epilogue   244

About the Author   250

Table of EFT Tapping Statements   *xiv*
Table of Prayers   *xv*
Table of Figures   *xv*

CONTENTS – EXPANDED

Introduction	**1**
What you'll find in this book	6
Spiritual Terminology and Concepts	**8**
Divine/Universe/Infinite Source/All that Is/Mother Father God/Goddess/Unity Consciousness	8
Higher Self	8
Karma	9
Third Dimension (3D), Fourth Dimension (4D), Fifth Dimension (5D) and Multi Dimensionality	10
Divine Timing	12
Chakras	12
The Aura	16
Kundalini	16
My Kundalini Awakening	17
Victim Consciousness	18
The Matrix	19
Energetic Implants	19
Entities or Attachments	20
Artificial Intelligence (AI)	21
The Shadow	21
Spiritual Empowerment	21
Negative or Toxic Power	22
Righteous Anger	22
Toxic Anger	22
Kinesiology and Muscle Testing	23
Part I Purifying the Bodies	**25**
1. Purification, and Why we Need to Purify in Order to be Radically Free	26
Part II Mental and Emotional Self Help Healing Tools	**29**
2. EFT (Emotional Freedom Technique)	31
1. Locating the Tapping Points	34
2. Be Specific – Priority Statements	36
3. Finding the Right Priority Statement	36
a) Finding the right statements – daily triggers	36
b) Feelings	36

CONTENTS

	c) Fear	37
	d) From Victim to Empowerment	37
	e) Trauma	38
	4. Muscle testing yourself	38
	Examples of further questions to refine your statement	40
	Reminders and further pointers	41
3.	ESR (Emotional Stress Release Technique)	43
	How to use ESR Technique	45
	Clearing day-to-day stress	45
	Clearing past stress	45
	Locking a memory into the body for healing	45
4.	Meditation	47
5.	Silence	50
6.	Prayer	51
	BE a prayer instead of praying	51
	Prayer of Gratitude	51
	Radical Trust	52
	Praying with Power and Authority	54
	Divine Synchronicity	54
	A note on prayers in this book	55
	A Prayer for Keeping the Faith	56
7.	Changing Old Stuck Limiting Beliefs & Negative Patterns	57
	Important question to ask yourself concerning negative beliefs and repeating patterns	58
	EFT example statements for negative beliefs	58
	Further examples	58
8.	Breathwork	60
	The Power of Breathwork	60
	What to expect during a Breathwork session	62
9.	Bush Flower Essences	64
10.	Dance, Yoga, Exercise & Movement Therapy	65
	Dance	65
	Yoga	66
	Exercise	66
11.	Getting Grounded	67
12.	Family Constellations	69
	A note on other tools and techniques	70
Part III Clearing Out and Purifying your Physical Body		**71**
13.	Healing the Gut	73
14.	Fasting and Detoxification	75
	Food intolerances	76

Refined sugar 77
Wheat 77
Cow's milk 77
Coffee 78
Soya 78
E-additives 74
Pre- and post-fasting 79
Variations of fasts that may inspire you 79
Lemon in water 79
A note on Salt 80
Soups 80
Juicing 80
A note on Flax Seeds 81
15. Detoxing from Heavy Metals 82
How to clear the body naturally from heavy metal toxicity 83
Zeolite liquid 83
Cilantro (coriander) 84
Chlorella 84
Burdock root 84
Bentonite Clay 84
MSM 85
NAC 85
Nettles 85
EDTA 85
Glutathione 86
R-Lipoic Acid 86
Garlic 86
Detox foot patches 86
Implementing new and improved lifestyle changes 86
16. Candida Albicans 88
What is it? 88
Causes 88
Candida and Kinesiology 88
Candida and Emotions 90
Cleansing the body from Candida toxicity 90
Anti-fungal herbs 91
Clearing Candida in children and animals 92
Australian Bush Flower Candida Cleanse Protocol 92
17. Parasites 93
Special Note 94
18. Electromagnetic Stress/Pollution 95
19. Auto-Immune Disorders 97

CONTENTS

20.	Healing the Hormonal System	99
	Healing the Pineal	99
	Healing the Thyroid	100
	A simple daily energetic balancing self-help tool	101
	Healing the immune system (Thymus)	102
	Thymus thump	102
	Candida, Parasites and the Immune System	103
	Exercise and Immunity	103
	Healing and balancing the Adrenals	103
21.	Reproductive Health	105
	Ovarian Health	105
	Healing the Testes	106
22.	The Energetic Body, the Aura & the Chakra System	107
23.	Detoxing from Media	109
Part IV Healing the Mental and Emotional Bodies		**111**
24.	Healing via our Relationships	113
	EFT example statements for our relationships	116
	A Prayer for our Relationships	117
25.	Healing the Heart	118
	EFT example statements for healing the heart	120
	A Prayer for the Heart	121
26.	Healing the Shadow	122
	Shame	123
	EFT example statements for shame	124
	Another example for tapping on shame	124
	A Prayer for Shame	125
	Judgements	126
	Healing our shadow in our dream time	128
	Astral Attachments	128
27.	Healing Past Traumas	130
	Trauma clearing method	130
	1. Think of the memory	131
	2. Lock it in	131
	3. Clear the Stress	131
	4. *EFT example statements for clearing trauma*	131
	5. Flower Essence	132
	Breathwork for clearing out conscious & unconscious trauma	133
	A note about psychoactive plant medicines	133
28.	Healing Sexual Trauma	135
	EFT example statements for sexual wounding	137

	STD's, infertility, impotence, hormonal disorders	138
	Sexual purification	139
29.	Healing the Inner Child	142
	EFT example statements for Inner Child Healing	143
	A Prayer for the Inner Child	143
30.	Boundaries and Self-worth	144
	EFT example statements for boundaries	145
	A Prayer for Boundaries	146
31.	Self-Love	147
	EFT example statements for self-love	148
	A Prayer for Self-Love	149
32.	Regret	150
	EFT example statements for regret	150
	A Prayer for Regret	151
33.	Guilt and Obligations	152
	Manipulative energy	152
	EFT example statement for guilt and obligations	153
	Some more EFT statements concerning guilt and obligations	154
34.	Clearing Fear Blockages	155
	EFT example statements for fear of being out of control	156
	EFT example statements for fear	157
	Phobia	158
	EFT example statements for phobia	158
	Embracing your fears	158
	Be persistent	159
	Food and fear	160
	Empower yourself	160
35.	Forgiveness	162
	EFT example statements for forgiveness	162
	A Prayer for Forgiveness	166
	From Victim Consciousness to being Fully Sovereign, free and empowered	166
	EFT example statements for victimisation	168
36.	The Divine Masculine & Feminine	169
	Healing the Mother Wound	171
	EFT example statements for Mother Wounding	173
	A Prayer for Healing the Mother Wound	174
	Healing the Father Wound	174
	A note on Anger	177
	EFT example statements for Father Wounding	177
	A Prayer for Healing the Father Wound	178
37.	Healing Ancestral Trauma Wounding	179

CONTENTS

38.	Healing Past Life Trauma	181
39.	The Ego	182
40.	Addictions	184
	The wonder of meditation and EFT	184
	EFT example statements for addiction	186
	Finding a new way of being	186
	A Prayer for Addiction	187
41.	Depression	188
	Natural solutions for depression	190
	EFT example statements for depression	190
42.	Living in the Present Moment	191
43.	Common Limiting Beliefs, Example Statements & Prayers	193
	1. "I'm not good enough" and the fear of not being good enough	193
	EFT example statements for not feeling good enough	194
	A Prayer for Not Feeling Good Enough	195
	2. "I'm afraid of my power"	196
	Negative power vs. Spiritual Empowerment	196
	EFT example statements for the fear of power	197
	A Prayer for Empowerment	198
	3. "I'm afraid of being out of control"	198
	EFT example statements for feeling out of control	199
	A Prayer for the Fear of Being Out of Control	200
	4. "I'm rejected and afraid of rejection"	200
	EFT example statements for rejection	200
	A Prayer for Rejection	201
	5. "I'm abandoned and afraid of abandonment"	201
	EFT example statements for abandonment	203
	A Prayer for the Fear of Abandonment	204
	6. "I'm a failure" and the fear of failure	204
	EFT example statement for fear of failure	205
	A Prayer for the Fear of Failure	205
44.	New Age or Spiritual Myths, False Light & Bypassing	206
	Examples of Spiritual Bypassing/False Light/ Spiritual Denial	208
	Fake Forgiveness	208
	"Turn the Other Cheek"	209
	"You are Projecting…"	209
	"We are all One"	209
	"Everything Happens for a Reason"	210
	"It is their Karma"	211
	"No Judgements"	211

	"Focus on the Light"	211
	"There is no Right or Wrong"	212
	"There is no such thing as Truth"	212
45.	Manifestation, Intention & the Law of Attraction	214
	Do what you Love	215
	Gratitude	216
	Abundance	216
46.	Triggering and Projection	217
	Meeting our emotional triggers as opportunities for growth and freedom	217
	EFT example statements for triggering	218
	Projections (A deeper understanding)	219
	EFT example statement for projection	220
	A note on Comparison and Jealousy	221
47.	Practicing Clear Communication (and How to Prevent Building Resentments)	222
	Communicating Clearly	222
	Listening	223
	EFT example statements for not listening	224
	Make no Assumptions	225
	Be Direct	225

Part V Clearing Out and Purifying your Spiritual Body   **227**

48.	Clearing the Spiritual Body, or Subtle Energy Bodies	228
	Energetic or astral parasites, deceased souls, entities and implants and how to neutralise these	228
	So how do we clear negative attachments?	229
	A Prayer for Clearing of Unconscious Contracts and Vows	231
49.	False Light Versus Unconditional Love	233
50.	The False Reality Matrix Construct	238
	EFT example statements for astral attachments	242
	A Prayer for Astral Attachments	243

Epilogue   **244**

| | *A Prayer for Humanity* | 248 |
| | *Final note* | 249 |

About the Author   **250**

CONTENTS

Table of EFT Example Tapping Statements
Negative Beliefs   58
Our Relationships   116
Healing the Heart   120
Shame   124
Clearing Trauma   131
Sexual Wounding   137
Inner Child Healing   143
Boundaries   145
Self-love   148
Regret   150
Guilt and Obligations   153
Fear of Being out of Control   156
Fear   157
Phobia   158
Forgiveness   162
Victimisation   168
Mother Wounding   173
Father Wounding   177
Addiction   186
Depression   190
Not Feeling Good Enough   194
Fear of Power   197
Feeling out of Control   199
Rejection   200
Abandonment   203
Fear of Failure   205
Triggering   218
Projection   220
Not Listening   224
Astral Attachments   242

Table of Prayers

A note on Prayers in this book   55
A Prayer for Keeping the Faith   56
A Prayer for Our Relationships   117
A Prayer for the Heart   121
A Prayer for Shame   125
A Prayer for the Inner Child   143
A Prayer for Boundaries   146
A Prayer for Self-Love   149
A Prayer for Regret   151
A Prayer for Forgiveness   166
A Prayer for Healing the Mother Wound   174
A Prayer for Healing the Father Wound   178
A Prayer for Addiction   187
A Prayer for Not Feeling Good Enough   195
A Prayer for Empowerment   196
A Prayer for the Fear of Being Out of Control   200
A Prayer for Rejection   201
A Prayer for the Fear of Abandonment   203
A Prayer for the Fear of Failure   204
A Prayer for Clearing of Unconscious Contracts & Vows   231
A Prayer for Astral Attachments   243
A Prayer for Humanity   248

Table of Figures

Figure 1   The 'Process' of Awakening   4
Figure 2   The Seven Main Chakras   13
Figure 3   Locating the Tapping Points   32-33
Figure 4   The Tapping Process   35
Figure 5   Muscle Testing Yourself   39
Figure 6   Clearing Stress using ESR   44
Figure 7   Steps for Trauma Clearing   46
Figure 8   A Simple Daily Energetic Balance   101
Figure 9   Steps for Trauma Clearing – a recap   132
Figure 10 Observing the Moment from Fear to Freedom   160
Figure 11 Using EFT for Forgiveness Work   165
Figure 12 Qualities of the Divine Masculine/Feminine &
           Father/Mother Wounding   175
Figure 13 How to Clear Negative Attachments   232

"Enlightenment is a destructive process. It has nothing to do with becoming better or being happier. Enlightenment is the crumbling away of untruth. It's seeing through the façade of pretence. It's the complete eradication of everything we imagined to be true."

Adyashanti

INTRODUCTION

Being 'spiritual' does not mean that you only focus on so-called 'love and light' or positivity. True spirituality encompasses the messy, dark and shadow sides of who we are too. When we no longer give our power away to others or allow others to manipulate or control us, and as we stand in full acceptance and love for all of who we are while taking full responsibility for how we respond to life, only then will we be radically free. True love and light is powerful and strong, and will stand up for the truth and what is right even in the face of great adversity. Love is fierce, wild and radically free. Everything in this book is essentially about stepping deeper into who you really are, your spiritual empowerment, your fearless boundaries, faith and self-love.

When I was younger I was terrified of making mistakes or failing, and I believed I had to do everything perfectly. Whatever that meant! These fears, coupled with low self-esteem, blocked me from living my life to my fullest potential. They also blocked me from expressing my truth to others in case they'd judge or reject me. So, I kept myself small for many years as that is what made me feel comfortable and safe. But once we commit to healing and awakening to our true wild and free authentic selves that lie beyond our limiting beliefs and fears, our unconscious will continuously, in manageable increments, push up what needs to be healed into the conscious mind, and what we perceive to be our daily reality. If we resist or deny what is being pushed up from the unconscious into the conscious we will get stuck in victim consciousness, or side tracked by distractions or addictions.

What the unconscious pushes up into the conscious for healing will usually feel uncomfortable or painful. If the heart or emotional body is blocked or closed due to past pain the feeling may also display as boredom, restlessness or numbness. These feelings, or the disconnect to ourselves, is what shows us we need healing. If we go into resistance here we'll block the healing process, but if we can accept and love ourselves right here in the pain, numbness or discomfort, we'll begin the process of healing and awakening. But how many of us can truly stay present and accepting when we're faced with our darker emotions, or with our past pain? We may be so used to pushing it down with distractions or addictions that we may even think there is nothing wrong with us, or we may believe that life is just a continuous struggle we need to push through. Either way we remain stuck, spiritually evolving at a snail's pace.

In this book, I'm going to be sharing with you some incredibly powerful healing tools that will assist you in your own awakening process. All of these transformational tools have assisted me on my own journey of awakening. I am going to be sharing with you how to purify your physical, mental, emotional and spiritual bodies so that you can embody the purity and power of unconditional love, which exists at the core of your being. This love, which is always there, unfortunately gets blocked and obscured by past trauma, fear, social masks, our shadow wounding (shame and judgements), limiting beliefs and thought patterns, and toxicity in general. This book will show you how to clear what is obscuring your *soul's gold*.

This book will show you how to clear what is obscuring your soul's gold.

The path of awakening to our true soul's essence and expression is a journey of letting go of the past, and an unfolding of our true authentic selves that takes time and determination. This PROCESS of awakening should never be shamed, as it is the only way to get from (a) our unconscious lower selves often stuck in the past, limited by the rejection of our shadow and fears, to (b) living from our hearts, embodying our higher selves and being authentically in the present moment allowing ourselves to flow within our natural state of synchronicity as we are able to radically trust ourselves and the divine (see Figure 1).

All the soul wants to do is to be free to express and co-create with Infinite Source. It will bring towards us exactly where we are not free in order for us to heal and become free. This explains why we can often repeat negative limiting patterns and make the same mistakes over and over again. We will keep attracting the same type of situations and relationships until we can work through the negative pattern or internal wounding thoroughly, learn the lessons at hand and free ourselves from its grip. Understanding this process of untangling from our negative patterns and past can really help us to heal ourselves with enthusiasm and a clear sense of purpose and determination.

In order for us to be *Radically Free* we need to have radical trust and faith that EVERYTHING in life has purpose and can bring us opportunity for growth. Everything! The quicker we can step into gratitude or acceptance for our learning, the easier and faster the process of healing will be. (At the same time, we do not shame others or ourselves when we find we're in victim consciousness, as it can take time and effort to get ourselves from victim into a place of empowerment and taking responsibility for our lives.)

It is important that we not only trust in life, but that we also trust in death. It means we are able to turn our challenges into learning so that we can expand and grow, and that we know that the toughest lessons we face will bring us the greatest opportunity to radically trust life, the Divine and ourselves. As we dive into the depths of our unconsciousness and darkness and bring the light of acceptance, compassion and unconditional love to it, we experience true soul alchemy turning our challenges into our soul's gold. This process can also be referred to as *self-realisation*, where we are continuously awakening to who we truly are underneath all of the ancestral and social or cultural layers of toxic shame, judgements and fears.

In order for us to be radically free we need to have radical trust and faith that EVERYTHING in life has purpose and can bring us opportunity for growth. Everything!

3

Figure 1: The 'Process of 'Awakening'

WE BRING OUR LIGHT

Higher Self

Our Light

(taking

responsibility)

- Consciousness
- Willingness to look at our shadow & bring love & forgiveness to it
- Heart-based
- Acceptance/forgiveness
- Presence
- Courage
- Feeling our feelings, i.e. our righteous anger
- Faith and trust
- Boundaries

TO OUR DARKNESS

The Lower Self

Shadow

(victim)

- Unconscious
- What we think we're not
- Judgement of self & others
- Shame around past actions
- Our darker emotions like toxic anger, shame and resentments
- Fear; whatever we resist will persist
- Struggling to say no or express/ shutdown

GROUNDED AWAKENING

It is imperative that we bring the light of our consciousness to our shadow wounding and traumas if we are to awaken thoroughly from the ground up. When we ignore our shadow and push it further away, as most religious and certain new age teachings teach us, by only focusing on the positive for instance, then we are bypassing and in denial and will be ungrounded. When we are ungrounded we are then easily duped by negative or false light beings.

In other words, to be in your true love and soul light you may have to go through a period of chaos. Where, bit by bit, you bring your loving compassion and consciousness to your shadow to integrate it deeply and thoroughly. This way you are *healing and awakening from the ground up*.

During our process of awakening we are consistently called to balance our inner divine masculine drive, strength and determination with our inner divine feminine that is full of softness, surrendering, nurturing and trusting. When we do the inner work, taking action (masculine) and surrendering into trust (feminine) we are able to shift and transcend our past at quite an effective pace. When, for instance, we are only taking action – neglecting our much-needed feminine ability to self-care and surrender – we begin to push or force life and ourselves for a specific outcome and block our own progress. Equally, if we become complacent and fail to take any action we will block our soul's growth. It is not always easy to keep this balance between our inner masculine and feminine, but with determination and a willingness to always go inward we can do it. Meditation teaches this balance between the masculine where we are taking action to sit still and focus, with the feminine where we are surrendering into the present moment. It is well known that meditation assists us in balancing the right (feminine) and left (masculine) brain, and is one of the reasons that it is such a phenomenally powerful mental-body clearing and purification tool.

Being radically free or awake doesn't mean we ascend outwards, or leave our physical bodies. In fact, it is rather the opposite, as we move deeper and deeper inwards towards our inner divinity and authenticity that is pure in our soul's essence and expression. One way of seeing our healing journey is that we are split and fragmented and as we heal we are bringing parts of ourselves back to ourselves while embodying it deeply into the physical body. There will come a time when we become fully soul embodied and integrated, once we've brought back all of our fragments in order to become whole again, and where the physical body can ground deeply into the Earth, in the present moment. Another way of looking at it is that we are letting go, bit by bit, of the past, the masks we wear, our traumas, resentments, regrets, guilt, shame, fears, social conditionings, and anything that stand in our way of being radically free, until we are able to be our complete authentic selves. Awakening can thus be seen as a process of *integration* and *letting go*.

Being authentically awake and soul-integrated means we're no longer living in a way where we are constantly triggered in the present by our past pain and trauma. In other words, we no longer take things personally. We're no longer giving our power away to anyone, or anything, so no more guilt and obligations towards others, and not allowing anyone to manipulate or control us in any way, shape or form. We're our own boss, sovereign and free from guilt and shame as we take full responsibility for our lives while living our soul's divine purpose. Being radically free means we honour our feelings, feeling them from moment to moment while expressing our truth clearly and compassionately. We love ourselves fully on all levels and thus have strong boundaries, as we honour our inner feelings and truth, what we want, and also what we don't like or want in our lives. From this Fifth Dimensional awakened consciousness, we naturally live our lives in forgiveness as we have moved through the process of forgiving ourselves and those around us during our awakening process. Remember though, that forgiveness – which is another word for empowerment – *before* awakening tends to be a process we need to work at. This process must not be shamed as we learn to work through our darker emotions like resentment, fear and feelings of victimisation.

What you'll find in this book

Forgiveness is an integral part of our awakening process, and is one of the many topics examined in this book. I will also be assisting you on your journey of integrating your shadow and inner child and teenager wounds, showing you how to accept and love your fears away, while building on solid, strong and firm grounded foundations. It is important to note here that feelings such as anger, grief and sadness are actually extremely important and part of our humanness. We do not lose these feelings when we're radically free. Righteous anger helps us to connect to our power, and to make necessary changes. Sadness and grief is also a deep expression or demonstration of our love and during our awakening process helps us to cultivate compassion. Once we're fully awake we will feel these feelings shamelessly, but they will rarely be triggered from our past pain, or if they are, they'll be processed without shame and guilt. These emotions will flow through us like a river in the moment instead as we allow ourselves to authentically express our emotional truth and power. To be *radically free* means that we're removing all the masks of social conditioning that we've been taught to wear from a young age while keeping our hearts open in compassion and love for our own unique 'messy' awakening journeys and for those around us too. Being at peace with our vulnerabilities and wearing our hearts on our sleeves while maintaining firm boundaries is a sure sign of spiritual empowerment and freedom.

In the following chapters, I'll provide a clear outline of how to safely purify your *physical, emotional, mental* and *spiritual* bodies, which is an essential part of awakening to our true soul's essence. Toxicity in the body is not only due to toxic food, air and water, but can also be stuck anger, resentment, guilt, regret, fear and any other stuck feeling or old traumas that have been trapped within the physical body due to suppression in the past. When we live in a toxic fog we are unable to see, feel, hear or know the truth from our important sixth sense or intuition. Toxicity in the physical body will shut our psychic sensitivity down from the truth of our multi-dimensional awakened nature.

Being at peace with our vulnerabilities and wearing our hearts on our sleeves while maintaining firm boundaries is a sure sign of spiritual empowerment and freedom.

The suggestions in this book will assist you in stepping deeper into your spiritual empowerment, boundaries and truthful expression. It is absolutely essential to understand the difference between false light that coerces with the dark by shaming us into a boundary-less existence, versus true empowered light where we won't allow ourselves to be manipulated or controlled, and where we also shine this light of consciousness and love on all of our shadow. In other words, we are not denying or pushing our shadow away where it will only fester and grow, showing its ugly head within our relationships when we least expect it. These are some of the topics I'll be examining here along with how to physically detox from heavy metal, parasitic and fungal toxicity in the body.

If you are ready to step out of victim consciousness into full spiritual empowerment and self-love, and you're looking for clear tools and guidance to do so, then you've come to the right place.

SPIRITUAL TERMINOLOGIES & CONCEPTS

The following explains the phrases, terminologies and concepts used in this book.

Divine/Universe/Infinite Source/All that Is/Mother Father God/Goddess/Unity Consciousness

The *Divine/Universe/Infinite Source/All that Is/Mother Father God/ Goddess/Unity Consciousness* I refer to in this book is your greater I AM presence, or All that Is, which is also unconditional love that encompasses duality and beyond. I see the Divine as myself and also as a far greater more infinite self. It would be impossible for my human brain to fully comprehend the vastness and infinite magical nature of the Divine, as it truly is unconditional and beyond all limitations. True miracles can be done from this unconditionally loving space as it is beyond the limitations of physical laws. It is everything we can see, feel, hear, touch and know and also beyond. I see God and Goddess in the same way. It is all within me, and then also reflected outwards into the life I experience.

Higher Self

Your *Higher Self* is that part of you that is working hard to assist you in your awakening. It is your own unique Divine Self that bridges you to All that Is or the greater Divine. Your Higher Self is of course a part of the Divine and is pure in its vibration and some believe it exists outside of the physical body above the crown chakra. I actually feel that the Higher Self is within our pure hearts, and the more we open our hearts the more we embody our Higher or Divine Selves to shine through. When we're fully awake we have fully embodied our Higher Selves in the here and now and our hearts will be open as we are fully soul integrated. I also sometimes refer to the Higher Self as the 'Budhic or Buddha Self', meaning it is that part of you that is already fully Enlightened and pure in the vibration of unconditional love.

Karma

My limited understanding of *Karma* is that it is in its basic sense the law of cause and effect. Whatever we think or do creates an effect, and so if we harm someone we will create a negative karmic reaction from the Universe/Life/ourselves to heal or fix what we've caused. Karma can either be resolved with a different person or situation where we learn what we need to learn so as not to repeat the same mistake again, or it will come again in another life with the same soul we had the original conflict with. This is why we sometimes meet people and almost instantly feel we know them, and then go on to have intense, sometimes traumatic experiences with that person. The reason for this is that the Karma between us wants to be resolved, and life will keep bringing us what is unresolved in order for us to resolve it.

To understand Karma, we need to understand that life is a part of us, an extension of us, working with us along our awakening journey. In the Christian tradition, they speak of paying for your sins. The original meaning of the word sin is 'to miss the mark'. In other words, when we're living or acting out of alignment with our soul and life's natural rhythms and flow. Life, as a fierce mother/father teacher, will always bring us challenging situations or relationships so that we can work it out for ourselves, and step back into our power returning to alignment.

To break free from Karma and the cycle or reincarnation is what radical freedom is all about. It means we no longer need to fix our past, whether it is from this lifetime, our ancestry or past lives. This entire book is filled with tools and ways to assist you in breaking free from negative past Karma and the reincarnation trap.

Your Karma is your own doing. If you remain in victim, you will never be able to heal your Karma, and this is why it is ESSENTIAL to take responsibility for our lives and step firmly and squarely into our spiritual empowerment.

Third Dimension (3D), Fourth Dimension (4D), Fifth Dimension (5D) and Multi Dimensionality

As we begin to awaken we will begin to sense and feel, see, hear or know that there are other dimensions of reality. Some of these dimensions of reality will feel so sweet and divine that we will be drawn towards them, while others may feel murkier or dark. For the purposes of this book I'll briefly give you a basic understanding of what I mean when I write about multi-dimensionality, 3D, 4D and 5D.

Third Dimension (3D)

The spiritual meaning of 3D simply means the Third Dimension of Reality. It is the *dimension of reality of materialism and the one we exist in, and all that we perceive to be real prior to awakening.* It is the reality of fear, separation and where the illusion of free-will exists. This is also a reality of the intellect, where most people will believe in coincidence rather than synchronicity. It is where the ego-mind needs scientific proof rather than trusting in intuition and flow. (But please remember here that we are always striving for balance between the masculine and feminine. If, for instance, we totally ignore our instincts and our intellect, we may end up in strange false light cults! We need to use our discernment coupled with our intuition, and our discernment will be strong only if we've made many previous 'mistakes' along our path showing us what is right or wrong for us. This is another reason why and how we can trust in the perfection of exactly where we are along our path of awakening.)

Fourth Dimension (4D)

The spiritual meaning of 4D – the Fourth Dimension or also known as *the Astral* – is where these controlling negative parasitic beings reside and where we can be manipulated unconsciously and also during our dreamtime. Many astral beings can observe us, but mostly humans cannot see or even sense these beings, unless we awaken to our multi-dimensionality. It is also the dimension where we can astral travel (waking dreams), and can be referred to as the Astral realms. These are the realms of the shaman, or of the plant medicines or where psychedelic drug takers may go to explore.

There are infinite light and dark realms within the astral, and if we have a lot of fear and have weak boundaries we may experience negative manipulation or attack here. Every human has an astral or causal body that overlays within and around the physical body. It can be very easy to get caught up and lost within the drama of the extreme opposites of the astral realms. The fourth dimension is the dimension where duality, light and dark magic, reign supreme. I have always found it interesting how in shamanic traditions they often will take on the entity or the sickness of the person they are healing, to transmute it from within themselves. This can of course be exhausting, and I've seen shamanic practitioners burn out as they work in this way, taking on the darkness of their clients to purge it out of themselves at a later stage. In my experience, even though this type of healing can work, it is totally unnecessary. We do not need to ever take on anyone else's negativity in order to transmute it. Many healers are also using so-called light beings from the Astral realms to assist them in their healings or channellings, and some of these beings are trickster spirits who also feed off their disempowered human hosts. I would advise to always heal from the Fifth Dimension, from the energy of unconditional love that exists within your heart. Also, the best healers won't actually give you a healing. They will simply guide you to heal and empower yourself.

Fifth Dimension (5D)

The spiritual meaning of 5D is the Fifth Dimension of *Unconditional Love and Awakening and is beyond linear time*. It is a fearless reality. (I am referring here to unconscious fears that stop us from moving forward. Of course, there is healthy fear that keeps us safe from falling off high buildings, etc.). Living in the fifth dimension is to be fully enlightened and radically free. We can exist in this dimension on the earth plane within our physical bodies, although our bodies will be far lighter and our DNA fully repaired and fully activated along our awakening journey. 5D is the reality of 'Heaven on Earth' and what we are moving towards when we follow the guidance of our higher selves and also the information within this book.

Multi Dimensionality

Multi Dimensionality is the ability to see through the veil of our 3D perception into the infinite multi dimensions around us, which includes the astral realms and also the Fifth Dimension of Unconditional Love. It is also being able to *tune into the language of synchronicity, metaphor* (signs and symbols in dreams and also in our waking lives), *and divine timing.* Also, our oversoul has various expressions and aspects like, for instance, other lives, that coincide with our current life here on Earth, but that are happening outside of linear time. As we awaken and free ourselves from the matrix control system here on Earth we begin to merge with our multi-dimensional selves.

5D[Fifth Dimension] is the reality of 'Heaven on Earth' and what we are moving towards when we follow the guidance of our higher selves, and also the information within this book.

Divine Timing

Divine timing is feeling the divine hand within time, and can be referred to when things tend to just fall into our laps or when magical synchronicity happens that guides us along our path to radical freedom.

Chakras

All humans have a chakra system of seven main chakra wheels of energy that corresponds to the body's endocrine or hormonal system. The Chakras are a part of our energy body and can only be seen by a few psychic people and also by Kirlian photography. We actually have many more chakras existing underneath and above us, but for the purpose of this book I'll only briefly explain the seven main chakras.

Figure 2: The Seven Main Chakras

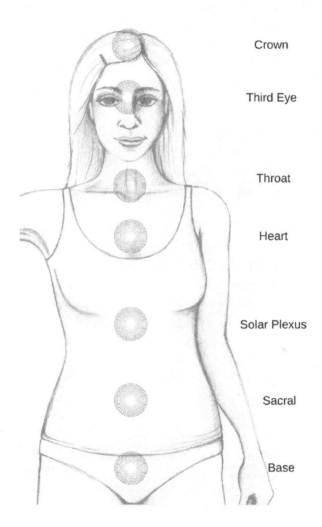

Crown

Third Eye

Throat

Heart

Solar Plexus

Sacral

Base

Base chakra (red/base of the spine)

The Base chakra is about safety, support and being grounded. If this chakra is out of balance it will negatively affect ALL of our other chakras. It is the FOUNDATION of the chakra system within and if our foundation is out of balance we'll be in fear, indecisive, nervous, feel unsupported, in victim, or spaced out in false 'love and light' New Age what I sometimes call 'airy fairy' land. Physically we may suffer back and bone related issues. When this chakra is fully balanced and strong we'll be in full faith, fully grounded and have trust in our path, the Divine and ourselves knowing that we're fully supported at all times.

Sacral chakra (orange/belly button)

The Sacral chakra represents our creativity including pro-creation. It deals with our sexuality (the *ultimate creative force we hold*), and also creativity in all other aspects of our lives. When this chakra is out of balance we may find we can easily get distracted and lose ourselves in addictions. It is therefore very important to stay within our creative flow. Also, when this chakra is out of balance we may hold sexual distorted energy such as shame or fear, and this may display physically as STD's, infertility, dysfunctions or cancer of the ovaries or testes, etc. Healing our sexuality and staying creative will help keep this chakra wheel in balance. Everyone is creative whether you think you are or not. Moving through your day-to-day is a creative act!

Solar Plexus chakra (yellow/hollow area underneath sternum)

The Solar Plexus chakra is *our power centre, our boundaries, strength and courage*. If this chakra is out of balance we'll be weak, have no boundaries or we'll suffer low self-esteem, and most probably be in victim-consciousness. When this chakra is fully aligned and healthy we're taking full responsibility for our lives and ourselves. We are unafraid to place our boundaries down in righteous anger. Righteous anger is healthy anger that is expressed for much needed change to happen. If this chakra is strong, people will feel your power and strength energetically and you won't be afraid to shine your purpose out brightly to the world around you, regardless of how others respond.

Heart chakra (green/pink/chest area)

The Heart chakra is all about *forgiveness, unconditional love, surrender and compassion*. It also encompasses grief, letting go and sadness. When this chakra is out of balance we'll be shut down emotionally, mainly in our mental body, the intellect. When the heart chakra is open and in full balance you'll be in forgiveness, unconditional love and compassion. You'll be expressing grief and sadness, love and compassion from moment to moment as you let go instead of holding on to stagnant energy.

Throat chakra (sky-blue/throat)

The Throat chakra deals with *expression* and when it is out of balance we'll be shut down, either allowing others to shut us down, or we'll shut ourselves down by failing to express how we truly feel. Fears, such as fear of judgement, rejection, conflict or abandonment will block this chakra. Imbalances in the chakra may display physically as thyroid dysfunctions or cancers and other degenerative throat diseases. When this chakra is fully aligned and balanced we'll express our truth from moment to moment regardless of how others will respond. We'll be communicating from our open hearts or fierce boundaries, either way, expressing what we feel is true and best for us in the moment.

Third Eye chakra (in between the eyebrows/pineal)

When our third eye is out of balance we may be either experiencing psychic delusions or more often than not will be shut down to our intuitive subtle psychic abilities. When this chakra is fully balanced we'll listen to our *psychic feelings and intuition as we flow in synchronicity* listening to the subtle signs of the Universe. We would understand how we're intrinsically connected to life and that life is a part of our greater selves, and so we'd be reading the signs of life along the way, knowing that we're being guided. We may have visions and deeper insights, and we'd be able to discern false light from true unconditional loving light.

Crown (purple/crown of head)

When the Crown chakra is out of balance we'll be cut off from our higher selves, the Divine and All that Is beyond our physical selves. If for instance you are an atheist and only believe in what you see here in 3D, this chakra will be blocked. When this chakra is open and in balance you will know and *feel your connection to All that Is trusting in the Divine*, and that you are a part of the Divine. Dis-ease and illnesses of the nervous system often relates to this chakra, and is the body's way of alerting us to deepen our trust and support in the Divine.

All the chakras work together in unison and if for instance Kundalini awakens it will begin to work very hard to clear out any distortions that may still lie within the chakra system. It is also important to note that you can purify your chakra system without an active Kundalini flow.

The Aura

The Aura is a field of energy that exists around the physical body. Some psychics can see it, and it can be seen with Kirlian photography. The Aura can get negatively affected when we go through emotional, physical, mental or spiritual trauma or physical accidents. To keep the Aura clear and strong we need to stay grounded and have a healthy self-esteem along with strong boundaries. You can massage your own aura if you've been through a trauma or accident with Rescue Remedy or any aromatherapy oils you may feel drawn to.

Kundalini

Kundalini is powerful spiritual energy that lives at the base of the spine and moves through all the chakras, from the base to the crown, that may awaken during this lifetime. Once unleashed it cannot be stopped. It is a fierce teacher, and its purpose is to purify the physical, emotional, mental and spiritual bodies while marrying the divine masculine and feminine energies within.

Kundalini Awakening has nothing to do with Kundalini Yoga, as Kundalini Yoga is a yoga practice. A Kundalini awakening is an experience that can be terrifying and/or blissful, and from my own understanding, experience and research, it seems to have a unique effect on each and every individual it is assisting in awakening. The reason for this is that we all have a unique soul history. In my opinion, this energy should never be tampered with, called in or forced in any way shape or form. Awakening this energy prematurely can be very dangerous and it is thought to be the cause of sending some people into mental institutions.

I've also spoken to people who have experienced seizures because of this powerful energy. It seems to affect the physical body's nervous system and may cause much pain, especially in the back or spinal area when unleashed prematurely.

This powerful energy has been teaching me via life and my Higher Self, how to authentically free myself on all levels of my being and how to step deeply into my sovereignty as a soul. It is mainly from my own experience with Kundalini and also the thousands of healings I have received and also given to clients in my Kinesiology practice, that I received deeper insights into our process of awakening. I will be sharing these insights with you in this book. My prayer is for this information to help you on your own path of awakening so that your own unique spiritual transformation may happen with ease and grace.

My prayer is for this information to help you on your own path of awakening so that your own unique spiritual transformation may happen with ease and grace.

There are different types of Kundalini awakenings. The Awakening that would be most aligned and safe would be the one that happens once you've first cleared out all of your old traumas, fears and spiritual impurities. Awakening Kundalini *before* purifying your mental, spiritual, physical and emotional bodies will cause discomfort and may involve severe pain, uncontrollable shaking or sounds, going into spontaneous yoga postures, spasms, itchy or painful chakras and other strange symptoms. Kundalini awakenings that happen before full purification of the body/mind are also often hijacked by negative astral beings making it extremely difficult for the soul to break free. I refer to the Kundalini purification process as Kundalini Cleanse, but I've also read that some refer to it as Kundalini Syndrome.

Warning: DO NOT CALL KUNDALINI IN! Trust it will come once you've done sufficient clearing and healing work. Awakening does not have to be a dramatic spiritual experience! In fact, it would be far more beneficial to aim for a more peaceful, grounded and aligned awakening.

Awakening does not have to be a dramatic spiritual experience! In fact, it would be far more beneficial to aim for a more peaceful, grounded and aligned awakening.

My Kundalini awakening

Before my Kundalini Awakening in 2013, I was the perfect 'love and light' New Ager who wore a mask of being overly nice while suppressing my rage and pain in order to be approved of. During my childhood, I used to observe my mother and other Christians like her doing the same and I called it FALSE LIGHT. Kundalini has helped me to differentiate between false and true light and to peel back this 'love and light' mask that lay over my messy, authentic, wild and electric self, and to step deeply into the truth and expression of my authentic feelings, power and boundaries. It has not been an easy ride, as Kundalini has brought me one painful lesson (via my relationships) after another in order for me to learn, grow, let go and free myself authentically on all levels of my being.

Victim Consciousness

Most of humanity is currently still in Victim Consciousness. When we're in Victim Consciousness we're blaming the world and those around us for our issues and problems. We are unable to take responsibility for ourselves or to look inwards to see where we may need to change in order to heal and grow. As we break free from Victim Consciousness we step deeper and deeper into our own power, taking full responsibility for our lives. We will naturally become more self-sufficient, independent and resourceful as we focus our energy on how we can solve problems for ourselves and in the world around us.

The Matrix

The Matrix, as in *The Matrix* film, refers to the false reality system or construct that is held in place here on Earth to deceive humans, keeping us distracted and in toxicity so that we can be used as an energetic food source for negative fourth dimensional beings. These beings have highly advanced and controlling technologies and humans are frequently possessed and also mind-controlled via TV, media, films, energetic implants, Artificial Intelligence and attachments that are unseen to the human eye. Artificial devices can be implanted in the energetic and or physical bodies of human beings to keep them locked in Victim Consciousness and toxicity, cutting them off from their natural FEELINGS, as we can only heal when we're able to feel. The Matrix can be seen as a false artificial mass collective dream or hypnotic state of disempowerment and enslavement. Humans are not at the top of the food chain as you may think. We are used as an energy source by fourth dimensional beings. The Matrix is this false reality system that keeps humanity enslaved by these beings.

Energetic Implants

There are hundreds of different types of energetic implants. Some of these can be implanted into the aura, chakra or meridian system, and some into the astral or physical body. Some of these are small and cannot be felt and others are larger and can be felt as they move around the body. Some implants are used for tracking, and others to suppress the physical body by putting strain on the immune or nervous system. Some implants can cause physical pain in the body. Many of these implants are able to drop thoughts in your own voice into your head to keep you trapped in misery and despair. This misery is an energetic food source to the beings who are enslaving humanity. Most people will have implants, even though they're unable to feel or see these. Some people, who've raised their energetic vibration high enough, will be able to feel, see or sense these. Yes, you can do a certain amount of daily astral clearing on yourself, but from my own personal experience you'll need to take responsibility and keep healing your shadow, trauma and fears within to keep these negative implants and artificial devices at bay permanently.

Some people believe we can be implanted with positive implants. This makes no sense to me as it is still a form of control. There are many false light astral beings that will pose as ascended masters, archangels, positive extra-terrestrials, spirit guides etc in order to feed off human energy too. Take care with your energy, your thoughts and where you put your attention. If you are confused come back to your own heart, the Divine within your own being.

Entities or Attachments

There are dark and false light entities that tend to work alongside implants and other energetic attachments, and can latch on to the human soul or even possess the physical body with its own dark or false light consciousness. When for instance people are very drunk and under the influence of alcohol, a demonic entity may enter the human body as they black out and will usually cause trauma and pain that the person won't be able to remember the following day. Also, people who smoke marijuana, especially GMO skunk can become split in their energy field and become easy targets for possession and implantation. I've seen this type of possession when someone I knew who smoked skunk daily for a few years, and who also suppressed trauma and pain, became schizophrenic and was placed in permanent care on anti-psychotic medication. They labelled her schizophrenic but I saw her head moving in a very strange way, eyes blank, and her voice change to a completely different frequency. During her 'psychotic episode' her soul had exited her body, and she was taken over by an entity.

But it is not only drugs that can open us up to possession. It is also violence, sexual and verbal trauma that can cause tears in the aura leaving us exposed to these darker astral beings. Also, as we Awaken we may become targets for this type of possession – especially when we have premature spiritual awakening experiences and still have shadow wounding and trauma in our field. I've been possessed a few times, and I can tell you now, it is a dark, heavy, nauseating feeling. I felt it very much in my physical body, as it felt weak and my consciousness heavy at the time. When I went through this I felt deep shame that I had attracted such dark energy, but now I feel no shame, understanding that this can happen to any person here on Earth as we evolve within these multi-dual, multi-layered, multi-dimensional reality systems.

Artificial Intelligence (AI)

Artificial Intelligence is everything from the invention of the telephone, the Internet and cars, to vaccinations and energetic Artificial intelligence that can also be implanted into the physical body in order to suppress its host. The real question to ask concerning AI is whether we have a CHOICE. AI can be wonderfully helpful and give an amputee a new arm or leg for instance. Technology is not all bad, but an important question to ask ourselves is whether we have a choice regarding it or not. When we are being manipulated, lied to and controlled it is of course hugely problematic for our soul's freedom and advancement.

The Shadow

The shadow is everything within us that we repress or deny, such as shame and judgements, and also our unexpressed gifts and talents. Every single human being on this planet has shadow. The shadow is what is unconscious, and usually what we project outwards as judgements. See more on Healing the Shadow on page 122 and throughout this book.

Spiritual Empowerment

Spiritual Empowerment has nothing to do with having power over others. To be spiritually empowered means that we're no longer giving our power away to anyone else. It also means we take full responsibility for our lives, and the choices we have made in the past, and the choices we make in the present. We no longer blame others or the world for our problems as we focus our attention on solutions rather than problems. We also commit to loving ourselves unconditionally while taking conscious action in the world bringing our dreams into reality. To be spiritually empowered we also need to be fully grounded and centred.

Negative or Toxic Power

Negative or toxic power is to have power over others via manipulation or control.

Righteous Anger

Righteous Anger is an anger that arises to protect the vulnerable and also ourselves from unconscious negative manipulative or abusive energy and attack. Righteous anger arises out of fierce love, and will rise up against the dark with ferocious power, like a lioness protecting her cub.

Toxic Anger

When we witness toxic anger it may make us feel very afraid of anger in general. This fear of being out of control and experiencing trauma may then cause us to push down any anger we may feel and then the anger begins to fester, becoming toxic to ourselves and eventually to others. If anger is unexpressed for too long we may fly off the handle when we're having a bad day and lose our temper causing harm and pain to those around us. Or if you are totally suppressing it, it will begin to harm the physical body, usually the liver or gallbladder. Toxic anger is fear based and feels incredibly out of control and scary. It may feel like an energy that takes one over and possesses its host. Often, negative attachments will feed off toxic-suppressed and also explosive anger that becomes abusive and harmful to those around us. All of the techniques in this book, especially EFT and Breathwork will be helpful in clearing out toxic anger from the body/mind. It is essential for us, along our path of awakening, to create safe space where we can express our feelings, our anger and rage and learn how to communicate our needs and truth in such a way so that we can avoid flying off the handle in the first place. I elaborate on communication tools and techniques at a later stage in this book to help with safe and effective expression.

Kinesiology and Muscle Testing

Kinesiology, also known as muscle testing, is a diagnostic tool that was discovered by a Chiropractor, Dr George Goodheart during the 1970's. Muscles will either strengthen or switch off and weaken when, for instance, various different foods, nutrition or even emotions are placed on or tested via the body. Each person is bio-chemically unique, and Kinesiology treats each person as the unique individual that they are. One man's meat can of course be another man's poison! The physical body can be seen as the unconscious computer of the mind/body system, and muscle testing shows the practitioner how and where to prioritise the healing. Sometimes a meridian system will flag up as a priority for healing, and with Kinesiology we can find out whether it is due to nutrition, emotions, structural or electrical issues. We can then use various tools and techniques to correct these imbalances.

Part I

PURIFYING THE BODIES

Below, in Chapter 1, I will elucidate upon why we are in need of purifying our physical, mental, emotional and physical bodies. Then, in Part II, I'll explain powerful mental and emotional self-help healing tools and techniques to be used alongside the rest of the information in this book. You may want to include these tools and techniques within your daily self-clearing practice to assist you along your healing process. The rest of the book is divided into sections for purifying the physical, emotional, mental and spiritual bodies.

Note
In this book, I will often refer to astral or energetic parasitic entities and attachments. From what I've been shown these attachments, which were referred to as *demons* by the Christians, *Djin* by Muslims, *Archons* by the Gnostics and the *predators* by Carlos Castaneda, feed off shame, trauma, fear, and whatever we suppress (our shadow). Most people cannot feel or even sense these attachments, but my Kundalini awakening opened my spiritual eyes to this controlling negative consciousness that negatively influences ALL of humanity and the Earth. In this book, I will share my limited understanding of this negative consciousness, how it affects humanity and what we can do to free ourselves from its destructive and controlling influence.

1

PURIFICATION, AND WHY WE NEED TO PURIFY IN ORDER TO BE RADICALLY FREE

Due to the false artificial matrix world that has been constructed here on earth most people are taught to automatically shut down their inner truth and authentic feelings from infancy. It can start with so-called 'sleep training' where a baby is left to cry it out in their cot, so that they can learn how to behave in a specific way. The message is clear, you can cry all you like, but we won't respond unless it suits us. We are told from a young age to stop crying, to be a good boy or a good girl. This good boy, good girl mentality causes our children to begin the process of wearing unauthentic masks in order to win our approval and the approval of others. If we are lucky enough to escape this kind of programming from our parents we are sure to get it at school, university or socially from our peers. Shame around our vulnerabilities usually takes a strong hold by the time we're teenagers, and the emotional, spiritual, mental shutdown continues. Every time we shut down our natural emotional response the energy has to go somewhere. Where does it go? It goes into the physical body, usually towards certain organs of the body. Unexpressed grief tends to go to the physical heart. Unexpressed or trapped anger tends to get stuck in the liver or gallbladder. Fear tends to go to the bladder or kidneys. And there the trapped emotions will stay eventually causing dis-ease, unless we are willing to clear it out authentically during our awakening journey.

On top of this emotional shutdown we are bombarded by artificial genetically modified foods, heavy metal toxicity, refined sugars, additives, wheat (a grain that has become increasingly irritable to our delicate digestive systems), and animal products where the animals are treated appallingly with antibiotics and inhumane living conditions. Our physical bodies become so dense with the toxicity of all these artificial acidic foods on top of artificial pharmaceuticals such as vaccines and hormonal treatments like HRT or the birth control pill, and steroids, that our bodies get confused and very toxic. Fungal, parasitic and heavy metal toxicity is a massive health issue for human beings on this planet causing many degenerative disorders and diseases. Even our water is contaminated with artificial hormones from birth control pills and of course fluoride. These toxins keep us disempowered, tired and enslaved to a broken body. We live in a daily fog, and we don't even realise that we're only half alive.

Not too long ago I was shown during a waking dream that most people on Earth are actually walking around shut down partially or completely to their soul's essence and soul's purpose. Human beings are programmed by 'the matrix' via media, advertising, TV, Hollywood etc., and enslaved by their own fears and disempowerment or victim consciousness to the point where they're cut off from their divinity, and are not being their true authentic selves. Our path of awakening is leading us to fully embodying our soul's essence so that we can fully express our soul's potential and purpose. Coming to life, being truly alive and awake in this way means we need to be willing to open our hearts and feel everything, but most people are too afraid to feel their grief, vulnerability and sadness and therefore unconsciously keep their hearts closed tight. There is so much trapped grief that needs to be grieved so that as a collective we can let go, cultivate compassion and move forward towards solutions!

We inherit from our ancestry negative mental belief programs that limit our expression here on earth. For instance, if your mother believes that men are unfaithful, and all of her partners were unfaithful towards her it is usually the case that her daughter or son will also believe that men are unfaithful or even act in unfaithful ways themselves. Unless they break through this negative belief pattern they'll repeat it and it will get passed down to their children. Our beliefs are incredibly powerful, and as we begin the process of shedding these negative belief programs we begin to free ourselves internally allowing for divine synchronicity to work its way through us. In other words, we begin to co-create with the divine to live our true soul's purpose rather than reliving the stories from our ancestral past.

One of the most prevalent ancestral and cultural disempowering beliefs we carry is that we have to work a 9 to 5 job we dislike in order to survive. I remember my mother urging me to do a secretarial course when I was 18 as she was convinced it would be the only way I would be able to become self-sufficient. Of course, there was no way I'd ever have done that, but many people are living in fear of survival, and this fear keeps them disempowered and trapped in jobs they hate. When we authentically clear and heal these mental belief programs and move into deep faith and trust in our spiritual path we will be provided for in all ways. This is spiritual law. If, however, we choose to stay in fear we will create more of that fearful reality of scarcity and lack. This is not to say that it is easy to break through these fears. It usually takes time to build faith and trust in the Divine that is unwavering,

As we purify we become lighter, clearer, more in tune with our authenticity, sensitivity and ability to set ourselves free as we merge our divine masculine and feminine energy within, stepping deeply into our spiritual empowerment and radical freedom.

Part II

MENTAL AND EMOTIONAL SELF-HELP HEALING TOOLS

The following self-help healing tools I have used on myself daily for many years to assist in my own awakening process. These techniques are incredibly powerful when used correctly and thoroughly in the recommended way below. Most of these tools I used pre- and post-Kundalini. I want to share these techniques with you so that you can be empowered and begin the process of freeing yourself on all levels. If you commit to your own awakening process and use these techniques daily coupled with frequent physical body detoxing, you'll quickly begin to see and experience real and lasting results. Don't take it from me though. Do it for you and see for yourself what happens.

Of course, there are many other self-help healing tools and techniques that I haven't discovered or used myself yet, and that are not mentioned in this section. I can only write about what I myself have experienced, and how these tools have helped me. Follow the signs and synchronicities of your Higher Self and life and you may be guided to use possibly some of these and some others you've discovered for yourself. The tools are only here to help and guide you to your true self. As soon as a tool or technique is being used to manifest or push or force a situation, like for instance a soulmate or a windfall of money, you know you're distorting the purity of the original intention of the tool or technique. Remember, we are here to free ourselves on all levels so that we can become fully human, grounded and centred, creating our souls joy and love. When we're pushing the Universe to work the way we want it to work we're coming from a place of control and fear. Always ask yourself whether you're creating from fear or from love, and follow the trail of love to your true soul's expression.

I highly recommend implementing a daily 30-minutes self-help healing program alongside a daily 30-minute or 1-hour meditation for optimal results.

If you commit to your own awakening process and use these techniques daily coupled with frequent physical body detoxing, you'll quickly begin to see and experience real and lasting results.

2

EFT (EMOTIONAL FREEDOM TECHNIQUE)

Emotional Freedom Technique (EFT), also known as Tapping, is an incredibly powerful, safe and easy to use self-help healing tool you can use daily to clear out your emotional triggers, heal your shadow and bust through your fears, to assist in forgiveness, taking responsibility and to clear out past traumas. There have been many books written about this powerful technique and there are thousands of free YouTube videos and websites that explore it in various different ways. I am going to share with you how I use tapping to clear out mental blockages and traumas thoroughly and deeply from the unconscious mind and also the physical body.

When using EFT we lightly tap various beginnings or endings of certain meridians while stating an affirmation out loud. A meridian, according to ancient Chinese Medicine, is a pathway through which energy, (also known as chi) flows. Each bodily organ for instance has a meridian pathway with an ending and a beginning.

As a Kinesiologist, I am able to muscle test for an affirmation that is a priority statement for my client, and I can also muscle test to see when the statement has been fully integrated or not. Kinesiology has shown me first-hand how important it is to tap in the right way. If I miss a shift on one of the points for instance the statement won't be fully integrated and the healing won't be completed. Then again, when we tap a statement that is spot on and we do it thoroughly we feel absolutely fantastic afterwards. As they say, the proof really is in the pudding.

Figure 3: Locating the Tapping Points

Priority Statement: you can either guess the best statement to tap for yourself or muscle test yourself (p 36) to see which statement is highest and best for you to shift and heal your specific issue. If you feel the shifts whilst tapping you know you have your priority statement.

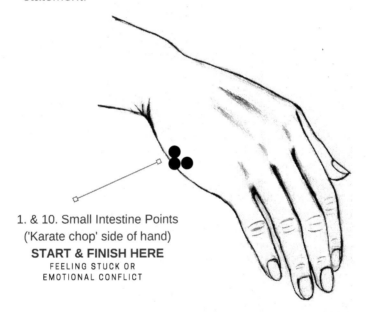

1. & 10. Small Intestine Points
('Karate chop' side of hand)
START & FINISH HERE
FEELING STUCK OR
EMOTIONAL CONFLICT

Tap lightly using both the index and middle fingers of either one hand or both (depending if points are unilateral or bilateral) starting at Number 1 and working through to 10. Stay on each point for a few minutes, saying your priority statement repeatedly until you feel a shift, then move on to the next point.

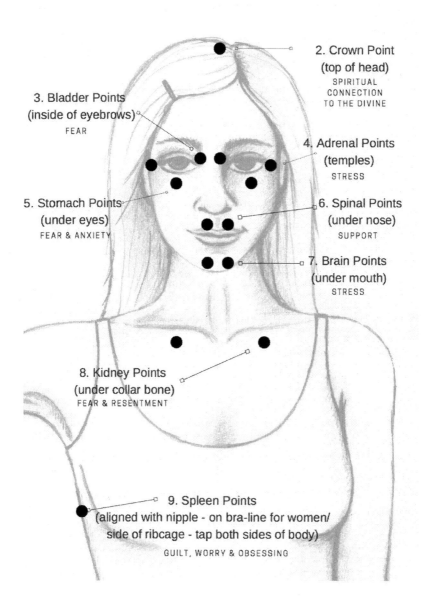

2. Crown Point
(top of head)
SPIRITUAL
CONNECTION
TO THE DIVINE

3. Bladder Points
(inside of eyebrows)
FEAR

4. Adrenal Points
(temples)
STRESS

5. Stomach Points
(under eyes)
FEAR & ANXIETY

6. Spinal Points
(under nose)
SUPPORT

7. Brain Points
(under mouth)
STRESS

8. Kidney Points
(under collar bone)
FEAR & RESENTMENT

9. Spleen Points
(aligned with nipple - on bra-line for women/
side of ribcage - tap both sides of body)
GUILT, WORRY & OBSESSING

1. Locating the Tapping Points

First of all, you need to know where the tapping points are – Figure 3 illustrates the points and Figure 4 summarises the process.

When we tap the specific EFT meridian points we tap with two fingers, the index and middle finger of both hands on both points simultaneously. We do not have to tap with a firm pressure. In fact, we can tap very lightly while saying our affirmation out loud or softly within.

EFT works wonders concerning emotional conflict. In other words, when we feel something we do not want to feel, or we're repeating a pattern we do not want to repeat, then EFT can be used as a tool to assist us in breaking free from the grip of the pattern by bringing the light of unconditional love and acceptance to it.

Whatever we resist will persist, and for this reason EFT works powerfully, as we love and accept what it is we're trying to push away or resist within ourselves. By bringing our love and acceptance to our rejected wounded parts we are integrating our shadow, and neutralising or clearing our negative emotional triggers.

Whatever we resist will persist.

For instance, if you believe you're rejected and you feel rejected by others, you'll attract relationships where you'll be rejected, as your soul desperately wants you to heal this pattern and belief program so that you can be free. Once you heal the wound of rejection from within you with EFT, you will not attract people into your life rejecting you any longer. And if someone does reject you, you wouldn't take it personally as you'd now love and accept all of you. Healing the wound of rejection can take many years though, even with the help of EFT. You'll need to be patient and very determined, always looking deeper inward and at your current relationships so that you can work with your present-day emotional triggers in the moment, in order to clear out these old limiting programs permanently. But it is worth the time and effort in the end when you break through as you're left with a feeling of lightness, clarity, freedom and joy.

Figure 4: The Tapping Process

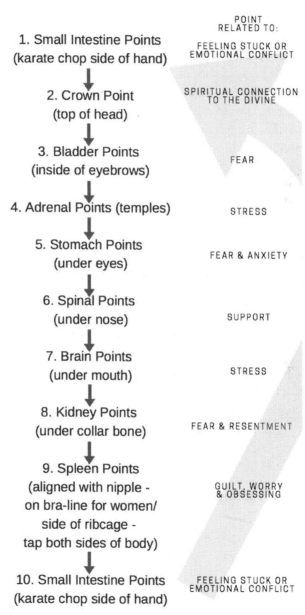

POINT
RELATED TO:

1. Small Intestine Points
(karate chop side of hand)

FEELING STUCK OR
EMOTIONAL CONFLICT

2. Crown Point
(top of head)

SPIRITUAL CONNECTION
TO THE DIVINE

3. Bladder Points
(inside of eyebrows)

FEAR

4. Adrenal Points (temples)

STRESS

5. Stomach Points
(under eyes)

FEAR & ANXIETY

6. Spinal Points
(under nose)

SUPPORT

7. Brain Points
(under mouth)

STRESS

8. Kidney Points
(under collar bone)

FEAR & RESENTMENT

9. Spleen Points
(aligned with nipple -
on bra-line for women/
side of ribcage -
tap both sides of body)

GUILT, WORRY
& OBSESSING

10. Small Intestine Points
(karate chop side of hand)

FEELING STUCK OR
EMOTIONAL CONFLICT

TAP EACH POINT LIGHTLY UNTIL YOU FEEL A SHIFT.
YOU MAY YAWN, BURP, SIGH OR HAVE A TUMMY GURGLE.
THESE ARE ALL SIGNS TO MOVE TOWARDS YOUR NEXT POINTS.

2. Be Specific – Priority Statements

It is always best with EFT to be as specific as possible when we create and repeat our affirmations. In other words, we tap on the actual memory, person or specific incident to get the best results. So, if we use tapping to heal sexual abuse trauma, we may need to tap on all of the memories we have first, and then after that, we'll begin to tap on our feelings, and when we're ready we'll begin the step-by-step process of forgiveness tapping, which is a tapping process I elaborate on later in this book (page 162).

In other words, we do not tap, *"Even though I felt rejected, I unconditionally love and accept myself"*, as it is too general and wouldn't work as thoroughly. You need to tap when, and by whom, you felt rejected. It would be a statement sounding something like this, *"Even though I was rejected by Nick at Sarah's party, I unconditionally love and accept myself as I am"*. EFT always works best when we work in the mode of a specific incident, feeling our feelings as we tap.

3. Finding the right Priority Statement

It is very important here to ask yourself what it is you want to happen, and then also, what it is you do not want to happen?

a) Finding the right statements concerning daily emotional triggers

Tapping on your daily triggers will raise your energetic vibration at an incredible speed. Let's use the example of feeling unheard during a conversation. You don't want to feel unheard, and you want to feel heard. So, you tap,

> *"Even though I felt, or was, unheard during my conversation with ..., I unconditionally love, accept, and hear myself as I am."*

b) Feelings

Tapping on our feelings can help us to let go of resentment, guilt, regret, trapped anger and fear. Here we start the statement with *"Even though I feel ... "*.

> *"Even though I feel angry/fearful/guilty/ashamed/resentful that Harry*

said ..., I unconditionally love and accept myself AND MY FEELINGS."

"And my feelings" is always added at the end of statements where we tap on our unwanted emotions and feelings. As we bring the light of love and acceptance to our rejected feelings they will drop away without any pushing or resistance. Tapping on feelings we don't want to feel, or feel shame over, is a sure way to integrate and heal the shadow within and also in our collective.

c) Fear

There are two different ways to tap on fear.

I.   You can either tap on the fear,

"Even though I feel really scared/afraid/panicked, I unconditionally love and accept myself, my feelings and trust that I am safe."

We always tap in safety or trust/faith when we tap on our fears.

II.   Another way of tapping on fear is to place yourself in the fear. So, say we feel afraid of being rejected by Tanya we begin to tap,

"Even though I am rejected by Tanya, I unconditionally love and accept myself as I am."

This way you're sending out a strong message to life that you won't allow other people's judgements or rejection to affect you negatively, and that you can stay strong in self-love and inner trust.

d) From Victim to Empowerment

Think of any memory where you felt like a victim and tap something like the following example,

"Even though I was a victim when Jerry shouted at me, I now take full responsibility for my life and I am grateful that it is teaching me boundaries and to stand up for myself."

37

In other words, we're not condoning what Jerry did, we are simply taking responsibility for ourselves and understanding that we can learn from what had occurred with gratitude. This type of tapping is incredibly powerful, pulling you out of victim consciousness into spiritual empowerment.

e) Trauma

We can either just tap our EFT points while talking through the trauma, or we can make a statement usually ending with, "*I now trust that I am safe*",

> "*Even though I was attacked by Sue, I unconditionally love and accept myself and now trust that I am safe.*"

Sometimes we can add in, "*I trust myself, life and the Divine*". Tune in with what it is you need to feel safe. Also, we can add on that we claim back any part of ourselves that froze or left our bodies due to the trauma, or any power that we gave that person or situation we can claim back with tapping.

It can be tricky to find the priority statement when we begin to tap, but with time and practice you'll soon find your way. You are also welcome to use a pendulum or my personal favourite, to use kinesiology or muscle testing to find the priority statement.

4. Muscle testing yourself

To muscle test yourself is not proper kinesiology, but rather to find a quick 'yes' or 'no' response from your own unconscious and conscious mind. The way I use this technique is to put the tip of my left thumb (I'm right handed), on top of the tip of my middle finger on the same hand to form a circle or hole. I then try to pull these fingers apart with my right thumb and forefinger asking for a yes and no response.

You need to make sure your legs and arms are uncrossed for this test to work properly. You also need to be well hydrated for it to work.

Don't give up when it doesn't work at first. I use a light pressure rather than a hard one, as this seems to work best for me. Incidentally when I muscle test my clients in my clinic I also prefer to work with a light pressure as I feel I am able to get more accurate results this way. Kinesiology and muscle testing is an energy test and a healing art rather than a strength test.

Figure 5: Muscle Testing Yourself

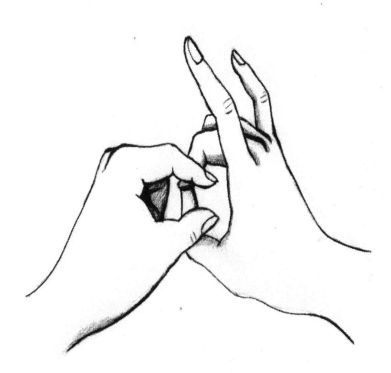

Always state your 'yes' and 'no' when using this technique before you test for a statement, to make sure your test is accurate.

Always make your statement in the present moment. Don't ask a question. In other words, if you want to know if feeling irritated is your priority statement, you'll muscle test, *"I am irritated"*, or for the EFT statement,

> *"Even though I am irritated today, I unconditionally love and accept myself just as I am."*

You'd then check the statement against your 'yes' and 'no' finger test. Now you can make the statement for what you want to muscle test, and then muscle test it to see if it will be a priority for you to tap.

Examples of further questions to ask yourself to refine your statement and to get it right

Example: Feeling disrespected

What is it that I want to happen?
I want to be respected, as my partner spoke to me in a disrespectful way.

What is it that I don't want to happen?
I do not want to feel disrespected.

How do I feel about what's happened, and am I ok with my feeling on it?
I feel disrespected and angry.

What do I need or what can I change within me for this pattern or behaviour to change in my life?
I need to respect myself to change this pattern of attracting disrespect.

So, your **first (priority) statement** will be as follows:

> *"Even though ... disrespected me when he/she said ..., I unconditionally love, accept and respect myself just as I am."*

Then follow with your **second statement**:

> *"Even though I feel angry that ... spoke to me in a disrespectful way when he/she said ..., I unconditionally love and accept myself and my feelings."*

I would then think of any other memories I have regarding feeling disrespected and tap on each one of these individually bringing in love, acceptance and respect for myself.

But be aware here that when we change patterns like these our relationships may need to change too. When we fully respect ourselves we simply will not accept others into our lives who disrespect us. If you are still tolerating someone in your life who disrespect you, the pattern hasn't been fully healed yet. Keep tapping on the triggers and eventually it will transmute the negative pattern.

Reminders and further pointers

Remember to be as specific as possible. Think of the details concerning your memory, and feel the feelings that it has brought up for you. EFT can clear or minimise the charge of feelings such as anger and fear very quickly when you tap with the priority statement.

Finding the priority statement is KEY, as you won't shift anything with an incorrect statement.

Feel free to exaggerate when using tapping as it can help to shift the energy even more quickly.

An indicator that you have the priority statement will be if you're yawning, burping, tears arise or you're feeling strong emotions, or having some kind of a bodily sensation at each point after repeating the statement for a few rounds. I would stay tapping on each meridian point until you feel a shift in the energy. It may take a few minutes per point. I usually yawn or burp, as my body will indicate the shift in vibration. Allow yourself to relax when tapping so you can tune into your body's sensitive responses so that you can feel the vibrational shift on each point. Sighing and tummy gurgles can also be pointers that you're moving energy and shifting your vibration. When you've tapped thoroughly on a priority statement you'll feel very light, free and clear afterwards.

EFT can clear or minimise charged feelings very quickly when you tap with the priority statement.

You can use EFT in a huge variety of ways. Another way I love to use EFT is to allow for my clients to express something they were unable to express in the moment while I tap their meridian points. This works exceptionally well when someone close to my client has passed away and they're feeling regret, guilt, shock or if they're stuck with unexpressed grief. Tapping their points while allowing for them to express their truth and feel their grief can be a deeply transformational experience, but needs tender holding from an experienced practitioner.

EFT can also be safely used to heal the repressed inner child. When the inner child experiences hurt and trauma and represses it, it will stay stuck within the physical body until thoroughly cleared out. With tapping we can go back into the memory and have a conversation with our inner child, ask him or her what he or she needs and then give it to him/her. This work is incredibly powerful, but works best with a professional healing practitioner.

You can also feel free to tap through a past story with no particular statement in mind. This can help to clear trauma from the memory, and it is very easy to do. Even though you can do this on your own, it certainly is best to work this way with a practitioner as having a witness to your healing can amplify it and help you to release emotionally while feeling safe in the hands of an experienced healer.

3

ESR (EMOTIONAL STRESS RELEASE) TECHNIQUE

This is one of my most favourite energy techniques as it is incredibly simple and yet incredibly powerful and life changing. If someone could bottle it and sell it they'd make an absolute fortune! But it is a FREE technique, and so most people do not know about its transformation power. Most kinesiologists will know this technique as we are taught it during our training, but many kinesiologists I know forget to use it too. I use it on myself, my family, sometimes friends, and definitely always on all of my clients daily.

When we get stressed in life we automatically tend to place our hands on our forehead. It is my feeling that unconsciously we are aware that there are these powerful points in between the eyebrows and the forehead that when held lightly can help us release stress.

When we use this technique daily it helps us to heal our adrenals. Many people suffer adrenal fatigue in our fast-paced world, and some of them even thrive on stress in order to get their work done. All this stress builds up in the body and eventually we become exhausted and drained. ESR technique will help you to manage your stress as you can clear it daily perhaps using the technique in the bath or right before you go to sleep as you lie in bed thinking over your day's stresses. It is wonderfully simple, yet leaves you feeling incredibly clear and free afterwards. You can also use this technique on your loved ones. I even used it when both my sons were infants and it always helped to calm and soothe them when they were distressed or teething.

Figure 6: Clearing stress using ESR

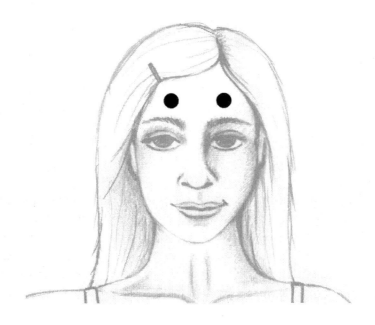

Lightly touch with index and middle fingers in between
eyebrows and forehead OR with thumb on one point and
index and middle finger on the second point.

Hold these points lightly whilst thinking of stress for a
few minutes daily. OR hold longer when going through a
stressful period. Hold until the mind feels clear.

*When we use ESR daily it helps us to
heal our adrenals.*

How to use ESR Technique

You can clear daily stress by simply placing your fore and middle fingers together on both hands and by placing these fingers in between your eyebrows and your forehead. If you feel a bit confused as to exactly where these points are you are also welcome to use your entire hand, and to place it over these points on your forehead. You can also use your thumb for one point and your fore and index finger on the same hand on these points forming a crab's claw to comfortably hold the points while lying down. See opposite (Figure 6) for more information

Clearing day-to-day stress

While your fingers or hand rests over these points you need to focus on your day's stress. Really get into the story and drama of it, and allow yourself to be in your head. When I hold these points for my clients I get them to talk to me about all of their stresses. After a few minutes, depending on how stressed you are you'll most probably begin to yawn. Once you have a really big yawn that is usually an indicator that the stress has cleared. You should feel clearer and lighter after using this technique.

Clearing past stress

You can think of any past memory where you felt stress in the body and use this same technique on that specific memory. I always use this technique when I do trauma clearing on my clients in conjunction with EFT and flower essences. To make sure you are working on that particular past traumatic or stressful memory, you can also lock the memory into the body before using the ESR technique. There are two simple ways of locking a memory or trauma into the body:

Locking a memory into the body for healing

1. The easiest way for me is to use my fore and index fingers together on both hands and to bring them together anywhere on my thigh and to then swipe a small area on my thigh with my fingers by pulling my hands apart while thinking of the

memory. I'd think of the memory first and then do the swipe while I have the memory in my mind.

This technique will ensure you're really targeting all of the memory. I would then use ESR followed by EFT and possibly Rescue Remedy if it was a really big trauma.

It is important that you do not move your legs while doing this technique or else you'll lose your lock. Of course, if you accidentally do lose the lock you can simply just lock the memory in again.

2. Another way to lock in a memory is to lie on your back with your legs spread slightly apart. You then think of your memory while bringing your straight legs together and then by spreading your legs apart in a fast motion. Again, you should not move your legs after you've locked in the memory, as you'll then lose your lock.

Once you have your memory locked in, even if you lose the memory in your mind while using your clearing techniques, it will still work as you've locked the memory into the body. With the memory locked into the body you can now use ESR, EFT and flower essences and give yourself a simple, easy, yet very effective healing.

Figure 7: Steps for Trauma Clearing

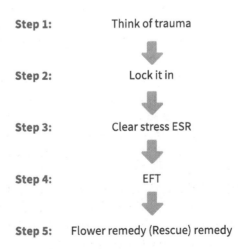

Step 1:	Think of trauma
Step 2:	Lock it in
Step 3:	Clear stress ESR
Step 4:	EFT
Step 5:	Flower remedy (Rescue) remedy

4

MEDITATION

Meditation is one of the most powerful mental body clearing/healing tools we have on this planet. There are of course various different ways to meditate. I love the Vipassana technique of body scanning, as it seems to really sweep the mind clear while instilling a deep authentic trust in the impermanence of life. I also enjoy meditating on the aliveness and the acceptance of what is right here right now by observation, and this would include the breath, my heart, the body, thoughts and everything else in between. Then there is meditation while doing, such as walking meditation or practicing meditation while eating or washing the dishes.

Meditation teaches us presence and faith in the process, while not taking our thoughts too seriously. When a thought would come up for further investigation, I'd make a mental note of the thought and I'd bring myself back to this moment, my breath or my body. I wouldn't do this with any force, but rather in peace, enjoying my mental clearing routine. Meditation will help you to understand your mind so that you can investigate your beliefs further during your self-clearing or inner healing time.

Going on a 10-day Vipassana silent retreat with up to 10 hours of meditation daily was a huge spiritual game changer for me. It is tough, and many people who sign up quit by Day 3, but if you can see it through till the end, the rewards of a clear body/mind feels immense. There was a time I meditated up to six hours per day. It is what I needed at that time. Nowadays I've been called to stop meditating in this way, as I was shown how I started pushing and forcing for an outcome. It is important to remind yourself that meditation is only a tool to help you learn about surrendering, trust and letting go. If you find yourself pushing, forcing or getting frustrated during meditation you're doing the opposite of meditation. Meditation is about integration, feeling peaceful and balanced.

When we meditate for long hours, synchronicities tend to speed up and amplify. After finishing my Vipassana retreat in 2014 I came back to the UK and was notified by my landlord at the time that she wanted to sell her property and that I'd have to find a new home. I knew that my higher-self wanted me to move to the countryside, but I didn't know where. I decided to meditate on this question. I meditated for two hours and when I finished I still didn't know where to go, but the phone rang, and it was an acquaintance that'd never called me before or since. "I hear you need to move, and I think you should move to Frome. It is apparently amazing for children and I'm also going to move there", I heard her say. I knew life was talking to me and I listened. That same night I was looking for homes in Frome and within a week I found my new home available the same day I needed to move out of my existing property. And the woman who notified me wasn't able to find a home there, as she was lead elsewhere. Isn't it funny how things work out sometimes? I was divinely carried from London to Somerset where I found myself nestled within the most awesome community of artists, free thinkers, musicians, healers, dancers and lovers of life. I stepped right into my soul community and family, and have never looked back knowing that this is exactly where I belong for now.

Meditation is about integration, feeling peaceful and balanced.

Meditation teaches us to balance our inner divine masculine, where we use determination and hard work to persist with our meditation technique with our divine feminine, where we surrender, yield and make no effort. It is taking action for non-action and also assists the left and right sides of our brain to be integrated and balanced.

The effects of using the tool of meditation are lightness, clarity and a stronger connection to the Divine.

5

SILENCE

When we are silent and enveloped in silence either on retreat or on our own at home, it actually becomes a powerful container that can amplify our healings and bring in divine synchronicity. Words are used to label and can more often than not get in the way of the truth beyond the label or wordy description. For instance, when we can look up at the sky and look at a large winged cosmic being gliding through the air, we may be degrading its mysteriousness by calling it a bird. The magic and the mystery of life can be taken away by labelling everything with words. Words can also be messy and confusing as we often misunderstand what others say or mean and vice versa.

At the end of one silent retreat I took part in, I felt clear and filled with love for all the people there with me. I also could feel their love and support for me. As soon as we started talking to each other on the final day I could feel the little labels, insecurities and judgements coming back in to my head. I could see and feel what was happening so clearly, and all I wanted was to go back into silence again! Words can often separate us from each other, whereas silence brings us an opportunity to connect more deeply with life, each other and ourselves.

6

PRAYER

BE a prayer instead of praying

Prayer can certainly assist us along our path of awakening, as it is yet another form of mental body clearing, while also strengthening faith in the Divine, in life and in yourself. However, eventually, once you've cleared out all of your past pain and traumas and integrated your shadow wounding you won't need to make prayers any longer. Once you're fully awake and radically free you will BECOME prayer in action.

Once you're fully awake and radically free
you will BECOME prayer in action.

Prayer of Gratitude

The most powerful prayer is a prayer of gratitude. Gratitude carries one of the highest vibrational frequencies and will help you to create the energy you are seeking. When we align with what we know is our birth right and we welcome it in and if we bust through all of our fear blockages that may sabotage our soul's authentic expression, then we are flowing in our natural abundant state as we connect with doing what we love. The trick is not to try, push, or force for a specific outcome. We simply connect with the energy of gratitude, faith and trust in God/ Goddess's/Life's way, not our way. "Let Thy will be done, not mine", is a powerful mantra that states our full trust in the Divine way. If our prayer is truly meant for our highest and best it will come to be. The clearer our vibration or mental, emotional, spiritual and physical body is, the easier it will be to align with what is for our highest and best.

> *If we still hold many unconscious fears and limiting belief programs we will unconsciously block our innate abundance by attracting our fears and limiting beliefs instead.*

Radical Trust

So, assuming we are quite clean and clear from our unconscious limiting beliefs and fears we then align with gratitude and faith, and if we do not get what we want, we automatically know that it was not meant to be, we would have peace for whatever the outcome would be. If we *do not* get what we prayed for and we're deeply upset, then we were coming from a place of *control, pushing* and *forcing* which is always *fear-based manifestation.*

When I was pregnant with my oldest son I was convinced that I was going to have the most amazing orgasmic water birth in my home. I did all of the visualisations, and I refused to listen to any 'negative' birth stories. I thought I was doing all of the right things to manifest my cosmic orgasmic home birth. Of course, as you can only imagine the Universe was about to teach me one heck of a lesson. During the birth, my body refused to open up most probably due to the past sexual trauma I suffered as a child, and after two days in labour there was meconium in my waters signalling that my baby was in distress and I was rushed off to the emergency room for a Caesarean Section. Crushed, ashamed and defeated, I felt angry at the Universe and my body for not playing ball the way I wanted. It took my body 3 months to recover from this birth as my spirit felt broken. In the end, it was a blessed learning, even though it felt incredibly tough at the time. It taught me about letting go and trusting in the Divine in a deeper way than ever before.

I remember a man telling me once that when his father died he felt so angry as he trusted the Universe to heal his dad, and that the

Universe had failed him. This is not true faith or trust. He had an agenda for his father to stay alive when it was his father's time to die. Imagine if we could trust so deeply in the process of life *and* death that we could actually celebrate and grieve someone's life absolutely knowing that it was their time to go.

Also, when Kundalini rushed into my life in 2013 after making the decision to leave my ex-husband I felt bewildered and abandoned by the Universe as the darkness descended into my life in quite a dramatic and fearful way. I thought I'd be rewarded for my bravery for stepping out of co-dependency, but the Universe had other plans for me. It slapped me hard with a fierce Kundalini awakening to speed along my awakening process. Instead of getting a reward of 'love and light' I was thrown into my shadow as darkness enveloped my life for quite a few years that followed. "God, why have you forsaken me" felt more like the prayer during that time. But thankfully deep within my heart there was always a candle of faith burning. This candle of faith guided me through the dark night of the soul and helped me to find the strength to find my true spiritual power, and remember Spiritual Empowerment is not a power we have over others. It simply means we're not giving our power away to anything or anyone, and that we are taking responsibility. I still had some traumas in my field, and I still needed to do a few years' inner work on my mother and father wounding while strengthening my boundaries and self-worth. Life, with an active kundalini flow, will not allow one to bypass what needs to be learnt in order to be truly and radically free.

The reason I share this, and the point here is to emphasise how important it is to keep the faith and to trust that your soul or Higher Self is always present assisting you in coming back into your soul's alignment. Sometimes our prayers are answered in ways that may feel incredibly challenging, but there is always a gift or a learning attached to any challenge we face. The sooner we can trust in the process and what is being thrown our way, the quicker we can heal what needs to be healed and shift into a new more expanded way of being. (But please do not say this to someone near you who may be going through a huge life challenge! When we're in the midst of turmoil we need compassion and space to work it out for ourselves. The last thing we want to hear when we're in pain is to find the learning or gift attached. The gift attached will come in its own time, naturally as we accept and express our pain in the moment, being gentle with ourselves.) What we may interpret as failures or mistakes are valuable learnings from our soul's perspective. The sooner we can pick ourselves up and dust ourselves off to move forward on our path, the easier the journey will be. When we wallow in victim consciousness we tend to create a blockage where we stay stuck until we're able to take full responsibility for ourselves and step back into our soul's authentic and natural flow. The easiest way to take full responsibility is to look at what you are learning, especially on a soul level, and to then integrate and embody this learning with gratitude.

Sometimes our prayers are answered in ways that may feel incredibly challenging, but there is always a gift or a learning attached to any challenge we face.

Praying with Power and Authority

When you pray, connect in with the power of your authority and prayer. Say the prayer out loud, or tap the prayer in if you feel you may be blocking it with your unconscious fears. Prayer is an opportunity to clear out unconscious blockages, so connect with the energy of gratitude and faith, then let go and surrender, watching how the Universe responds. If you get more of your fears, then that is what needs to be cleared. Trust even that! You may be totally surprised and be given something so much more spectacular than you could ever have imagined. And remember that you are always being given an opportunity for healing when you face challenge.

Divine Synchronicity

Prayer is also asking a question to the Universe out loud, and then letting go, only to have your prayer answered when you least expect it via synchronicity. I use prayer in this way ALL the time. This is how you can integrate prayer into your day-to-day and begin to have a conversation with life and your Higher Self. Shortly after my awakening in 2013, I went for a run in my local park. I asked the question whether I was fully awake yet in my head and came to a zebra crossing. There were two other women also jogging and waiting alongside me. One of them was clearly annoyed with the traffic at the crossing, while her friend responded, "*Just be patient, and you'll soon be able to cross*". For me, this was an instant answer to my prayer. And this type of dialogue with life is always happening if only we're willing to pay attention. The answer to your prayer may be in the lyrics of a song you happen to hear on radio, or a bird flying nearby or even a word that jumps out at you on the back of a truck while you're driving! You can turn your entire life into a prayer by connecting to synchronicity and reading the signs, or answers to prayer in this way.

When we speak a prayer out loud it can be very powerful indeed as you're sending a clear message to your unconscious mind. The more you can connect in with your own authority and inner faith the more powerful the prayer will be for you. When we pray to "*Mother Father Divine, Universe, Unconditional Love, I Am Presence*", or however you'd like to call on the Divine, please remember that you are actually only calling in a greater aspect of YOURSELF!

A note on prayers in this book

You will find example prayers throughout this book for you to use as a guideline in your own daily practice. Remember that prayer is a way of connecting with your Higher Self and All that Is, creating a feedback loop via synchronicity. You can practice the suggested prayers and eventually create your own ones to express out loud with authority in your voice. Feel the power of your prayer and totally let go once you're done. Give space in your life for your prayers to be answered as more often than not they'll be answered in ways you would not expect. Be open to hearing, seeing or feeling the signs along your daily path that are leading you ever inward towards your true liberated and radically free self.

A Prayer for Keeping the Faith

"Mother Father Divine within, Unconditional Love, I Am Presence,

thank you for assisting me on my spiritual path and for being within and around me at all times. Thank you for bringing me what it is I need to awaken. I have deep faith and trust in my path, and know that I am exactly where I am meant to be right now. Thank you for guiding me. I am listening and will follow the signs, and listen to my feelings and intuition as I strengthen my trust and faith in myself and in the process of life. I am deeply grateful for your full support and unconditional love.

It is done, and so it is. Aho/Amen/Thank You."

7

CHANGING OLD STUCK LIMITING BELIEFS AND NEGATIVE PATTERNS

Human beings are extremely powerful and the thoughts we think and the words we say can hold incredible power over others and ourselves. If we keep feeding our consciousness with negative thoughts and beliefs then we'll be stuck in that vibration until we decide to change it. EFT can be incredibly powerful for changing beliefs.

The great news is that you can change your beliefs. You can use your belief or faith in the Divine to clear out the negative stuck belief programs, and you can exchange the negative, limiting thought or belief for a new empowered one. You can simply do this by expressing it out loud and knowing that it is done, or you can use tapping to install the new belief deeply within the unconscious mind. You can also use muscle testing to test and see if you've cleared the belief program (as explained in Chapter 2, page 38). Beliefs can also be changed and healed via prayer, meditation and visualisation. The important thing here to remember is that you need to believe the new belief and that you then need to live your new belief, putting it into action in your day to day reality.

Muscle test yourself to see if the new belief has integrated, and trust what life brings you in order to shift, change and grow.

Important question to ask yourself concerning negative beliefs and repeating patterns

Ask yourself,

> "How does this negative belief pattern serve my soul? What has it been teaching me? Or what is it that my soul wants to learn from this experience?"

Usually the soul wants to learn the opposite of what is showing up in the negative. For example, if you keep attracting untrustworthy relationships it may be serving you by teaching you to be more trustworthy, how to love and accept yourself and how to stand up for yourself.

EFT example statements for negative beliefs

Here you can tap the following example statement:

> "Even though … has broken my trust when …, I unconditionally love and accept myself and am grateful that I have now learnt the lesson of being a trustworthy person while standing up for myself."

You'll need to tap on all of your memories individually where your trust was broken, bringing in for yourself what your soul really wants to learn so as to shift and heal this pattern from deep within your psyche.

Further examples

If, for instance, you keep attracting men who disrespect you, you most probably hold an unconscious belief that men are disrespectful towards women, and that men also disrespect you. You can change these beliefs with EFT in the following statements:

> "Even though men, my father, my brother, my husband, etc disrespect women and myself, I unconditionally love and accept and respect myself just as I am."

"Even though I am disrespected by this man when he did or said ... [be as specific as possible], *I unconditionally love, accept and respect myself as I am."*

This can of course also apply to feeling disrespected by women.

Once you've brought in the respect for yourself from yourself you won't allow for others to treat you in a disrespectful way. In other words, disrespectful relationships will fall away naturally once you respect yourself. It really is as simple as that. But with deep-seated patterning and programs you may have to tap on all of your conscious memories around being disrespected to root it out very deeply and thoroughly. It really depends on how deeply rooted the program is.

Usually the soul wants to learn the opposite of what is showing up in the negative.

8

BREATHWORK

I discovered Breathwork only after my Kundalini was already actively cleansing and purifying my emotional, mental, physical and spiritual bodies. Kundalini guided me to the breath synchronistically and I was totally amazed at the power of the breath. Rebirthing, which is a well-known breathing technique in the West was apparently birthed out of Kriya Yoga. Kriya Yoga was of course taught to the disciples of guru's and Yogi's in India for centuries as part of their training for enlightenment.

The Power of Breathwork

Breathing in a deep, rhythmic and continuous way, either through the nose or through the mouth cleanses and purifies the emotional body, and it can be extremely powerful. It needs to be handled with care and compassion by an experienced space holder so that you can feel safe enough to really let go of your trapped stuck emotions. The breath will get you there if you are willing to do the work and breathe in the instructed way. I cannot recommend Breathwork enough. During my second transformational breath session I cleared my birth trauma. I sobbed for a very long time, and my breath practitioner eventually picked me up and held me in her arms. I felt like a newborn baby, light as a feather crying out all of the pain of coming into this world and being separated from my mother.

There are a variety of Breathwork modalities such as Rebirthing, Transformational breath, Clarity Breathwork and Holotropic breathing.

You can do Breathwork on your own, but I would advise to first start with an experienced practitioner for at least 10 sessions. Also having a witness during the healing process right there with you will help you to release any pent up or trapped emotions. With the right practitioner you will be guided with compassion and love, as you release what no longer serves you. After a huge emotional release, I always felt filled up with incredibly life energy. I would go dancing afterwards or come home and do yoga, as I'd feel the urge to move my body in its new lighter vibration. Breathwork tears are similar to grief tears. When we grieve, our tears are also deeply cleansing, as each tear will help us to let go ever deeper from the past, allowing us to feel cleansed, pure and light afterwards.

> *As we awaken we need to toughen up so that we can become totally ok with our fierceness, our truth and our boundaries.*

Many of us are taught to wear a mask of being overly nice for approval, often at the expense of our true feelings. This overly nice mask we wear is a clear sign of FALSE light that can be seen in all religions including the New Age and is also deeply embedded within our culture too. Most people are wearing masks, and they have worn these masks for so long they may even believe the mask is who they truly are! As we awaken we need to toughen up so that we can become totally ok with our fierceness, our truth and our boundaries. We need to become totally ok with being disliked, misunderstood, judged or rejected. Imagine if we could teach our children to be stronger within their own boundaries and self-esteem? When a child has low self-worth and they're wearing this mask of having to be nice to grown-ups and everyone around them, they can become easy targets for sexual, emotional or physical abuse. A paedophile wouldn't prey off a child who is empowered and ok to exert their boundaries. I want my children to have kick ass boundaries! I don't care if it seems disrespectful towards an adult. Adults need to understand that children have rights too, and it is their basic human right to say no, stop, I don't like you/this, leave me alone or go away.

Honouring our feelings in the moment and expressing our truth with those around us will assist us in the process of allowing our emotional body to flow. The emotional body needs to flow like a river in order for us to be truly healthy and free.

When we're fully awake we will still feel sadness, anger and grief, but it will be felt in the present moment, and authentically expressed, in order to be released in a healthy way. The reason we can feel fearful around the expression of our anger is because we've bottled it up and then lose our temper, or we've seen others lose their tempers and cause huge upset or trauma. It may take time to trust that it is safe to express our anger in a healthy way. I get my kids to stomp out their anger, and we usually end up in fits of laughter after having a pillow fight or a good roll around on the bed. Children need to be shown how natural and normal it is to express these big scary feelings in a healthy way. Also, when my children cry I know I am being called to step into my compassionate heart and to stay present for and with them. I have to admit; this can be very challenging at times, especially when there have been many tantrums in the day. Sometimes I just want to walk away and say enough! And I've certainly done that before, but I know that the best way of dealing with small children with big feelings is to stay patiently unconditionally loving while also expressing my boundary as their parent in a consistent way.

Breathwork assists us to clear out all of our stuck and trapped emotions, and the process will automatically help us to express our emotions in a healthy way during our day-to-day, keeping our physical bodies healthy too.

What to expect during a Breathwork session

Breathwork is hard work! Some Breathwork requires us to breathe through the nose, and some through an open mouth. You'll need to stay focused for at least an hour while you breathe very deep connected breaths, meaning there are no pauses between your in and out-going breaths. You will be breathing in a lot more oxygen or prana (life force energy) than you usually do while lying on your back. Often one can experience spasms, heat and cold within the body, accompanied by authentic emotional outbursts.

After your breath session you'll feel much lighter and clearer.

Please only attempt this on your own after seeing an experienced practitioner for at least 10 sessions.

9

BUSH FLOWER ESSENCES

I love the subtle power of flower remedies. My personal favourite essences that I tend to work with on my children, my clients, and myself are the Australian Bush Flower Remedies. There are 69 flower essences in this range, and they all work on various different emotional blockages. Using Bush Remedies intuitively or using muscle testing to see what we need always amazes me when the exact essences we need will always show up. I've experienced and seen many miraculous shifts with these essences. When I was first introduced to them I thought it might be placebo, and I was ok with placebo too, as I find placebo miraculous in itself, but very quickly I was shown with Kinesiology that these vibration essences actually really do heal specific emotional imbalances. And often once the emotional imbalances have been healed the physical body can heal too.

Purifying Essence: *Purifying Essence* is an Australian Bush Flower Combination Remedy that I've been working with over the past 13 years, and it has become one of my staples I go to when I purify and detox. It is incredibly powerful and can even change one's bowel movements as it assists us in brushing out the past, letting go of unconscious resentments, anger, bitterness, etc.

The Bush Flower Essences are expanded on elsewhere in this book, and page 92 details the protocol using the Bush Flower Essences for clearing Candida in children and animals.

10

DANCE, YOGA, EXERCISE AND MOVEMENT THERAPY

Dance

When we can allow our bodies to flow according to their natural rhythm, expressing ourselves shamelessly to a variation of emotive music, such as in a 5 Rhythms class, we are able to move pent-up energy out of the body/mind through our unique authentic movement. Dancing our unique dance, expressing our inner truth in this way can allow for us to drop deeply into the body and to release trapped emotions we may have held onto for a very long time. I have found myself in floods of tears many times during dance and movement classes. It is of course important that we feel safe within the group, so we may not be able to have a big emotional release if we are new to a class. Although, of course this can sometimes be exactly what we need to release among strangers who can hold us or allow for us to just be in our vulnerability.

Dance teaches us how to let go and trust on a very deep level, and movement can really allow for us to express our inner unconscious selves. I use dance at the end of my week to let go of all the holding I do with my children and clients during the week. It has become important weekly medicine for my soul, and I feel deeply grateful that I have such a tight-knit community around me where I can feel safe to release in any which way I need. Sometimes we make noise, sometimes we cry, roll around on the floor, rage, howl at the moon, shake and of course we always dance. It has become a space for us to lose our inhibitions, and where we can get really naked in our dance to freedom. It feeds my spirit and brings me so much joy, even when I'm processing through heavy darkness.

Dance your own unique dance, get your mind out the way, and allow for your body to express its truth. Music and dance can bring us profound healing! It is also incredibly grounding, and can assist us in feeling safe and supported.

> *Dance your own unique dance, get your mind out the way, and allow for your body to express its truth.*

Yoga

I'm not sure if you're familiar with the expression, 'yoga tears'. I've had many yoga tears during yoga sessions where I'd sink into a posture, usually a heart opening one and within that stretch I'm able to unlock some deep collective or ancestral grief. I usually never know why I'm crying, but I trust in the process of the release as it happens in the moment. Sometimes people worry or project their own thoughts onto what I'm processing, more so during yoga, than the dance, but I'm ok with that. It feels like it may be good medicine for others to witness my grief, and on another level, I am giving them permission to grieve too. The more we can get in touch with our own grief the greater the capacity will be for us to have compassion and to love others unconditionally.

Exercise

Any type of exercise will help us move energy throughout the physical body, bringing oxygen to the brain. Even if you are unable to exercise due to illness or old age, just to do what you can in order to move your limbs and to get your energy or chi to flow. A strong body often accompanies a strong mind and spirit.

11

GETTING GROUNDED

What does it really mean to be grounded? Being grounded and centred within our physical body means we're present, aware and conscious with our feet firmly planted on the earth. It means we're trusting in the process of life, the Divine and ourselves.

When we're ungrounded, we're in fear, panic, nervousness, stress, or scattered, all over the place, in a fog, bumping into things, having accidents and generally acting out of alignment or feeling detached from our physical bodies.

Eating root vegetables, receiving bodywork such as massage, exercise, walking barefoot on grass, sleeping on earthing sheets, and dance can help us to ground temporarily, but we won't ground very deeply unless we've addressed and healed the root cause of why we're in an ungrounded state. The root cause may be a fear, usually due to a previous trauma. At the same time, I would still advise to do grounding activities, as they tend to be very healing and helpful for us, especially spending time in nature. Nature can sweep away the mental cobwebs, clear fear and assist us in grounding very powerfully.

Nature can sweep away the mental cobwebs, clear fear and assist us in grounding very powerfully.

The best way to ground from my own experience is to clear your fear with *EFT* and by *tapping* in safety! (for a reminder see Chapter 2, page 31). When we are rooted in faith and trust ALL IS WELL despite whatever is happening. We will then be grounded on firm foundations, and our root chakra will be balanced.

Using the *ESR stress release technique* (page 44) coupled with deep inhalations and exhalations can also help us to get centred and grounded. Remember to focus your energy on the problem while using ESR.

You can of course also *meditate* while focusing on roots growing out of your feet into the Earth centring and grounding you. Or, one of my personal favourites, focus your energy on the gravitational pull of the Earth and imagine it as mother Earth anchoring and hugging you safely with unconditional love.

Flower Essences can also help us to get grounded and centred.

Physical exercise is of course immensely grounding and good for our physical, mental, emotional and spiritual bodies. When we exercise we are breathing more deeply, bringing more oxygen to the cells in our bodies. We are also gaining strength and stamina on ALL levels of our being. This is one of the reasons we feel so good after we've exercised. Physical exercise can also clear out stress and mind clutter. Cardiovascular exercise in particular is fantastic for helping us get grounded and centred.

12

FAMILY CONSTELLATIONS

Family Constellations is a healing modality birthed out of psychotherapy and drama therapy. It is a technique that has to be experienced one-to-one with a professional practitioner or within a group setting held by a professional Family Constellations Practitioner. Family Constellation sessions can be immensely powerful and help clear out old trauma, negative family patterns and pain. This work helped me to clear out some deep unexpressed trapped grief concerning my ex-husband that I really had no idea was still even there. I find doing EFT after a family constellations session very helpful to clear out anything that may have been brought to the surface for further investigation and healing.

A note on other tools and techniques

Please remember that there are many other tools that may be able to also assist you in becoming a fearless and grounded human being. Follow your unique soul's path and use what you feel drawn to in these pages while discarding what doesn't resonate. You may be guided to do somatic healing, hypnosis, Eye Movement Desensitisation and Processing (EMDR), or other modalities, and I have heard many wonderful things about these techniques and others. Keep following your own inner guidance to explore, let go and integrate in order for you to be radically free.

Part III

CLEARING OUT AND PURIFYING YOUR PHYSICAL BODY

Our physical bodies need to be clear of toxins and fully grounded and centred in order to be the strong vessel for our soul and spirit to shine through. If we are genuinely willing to listen to the aches and pains of our physical bodies then we will begin to hear they have their own unique language that relay information about what is going on with our mental/emotional/spiritual bodies. Often when we heal emotional issues our physical bodies may also begin to heal. And often when we heal our physical bodies our emotional issues may begin to heal. They really do work hand in hand. Your body is your spiritual temple and deserves to be treated with loving kindness and care.

A huge part of our awakening journey encompasses detoxification. In fact, we are continuously detoxing our physical, emotional, mental and spiritual bodies as we heal and become fully soul embodied. Trapped, stuck emotions and limiting negative beliefs are highly toxic to our physical bodies. I've often experienced a spontaneous physical body detox after doing spiritual, mental or emotional body healing.

As our spiritual vibration increases our body will show us where to make changes. Our children may tell us that they don't want to eat meat, or our bodies simply won't be able to digest certain foods any longer. Toxins are often encased within fat cells, and we need to break down these fat cells safely in order to detoxify and release any excess weight.

At the same time, it is very important to note that we do not need to be thin, healthy and super fit in order to awaken! We are not striving for perfection here. We are simply letting go of old toxic energy safely and at our own individual pace.

This entire book is explaining in depth how to detox and purify yourself on all levels of your being so that you can be radically free.

13

HEALING THE GUT

When the gut is out of balance it will lower the body's immunity and may also cause adrenal fatigue, thyroid imbalances, endocrine-related health issues, and other degenerative and chronic or inflammatory disorders. The gut, and very specifically the small intestine in its natural healthy state have a balance of good and bad bacteria. When this balance is compromised and negative funguses or parasites become overgrown causing an imbalance, then our delicate internal ecosystem becomes toxic and acidic and if this continues for longer than three months it usually migrates from the gut to the rest of the body and becomes systemic. Within this process of migration, the physical body would experience what is known as Leaky Gut, and this may also cause various food intolerances or confused autoimmune responses as the body's immune system becomes compromised. All these toxins swimming within the body cause one to become hyper-sensitive to chemicals while lowering the spiritual vibration, keeping one in a fog, disempowered and enslaved in victim consciousness.

From my experience as a Kinesiologist, working with thousands of different clients, I've seen how each person will have a weak spot in the physical body. My weak spots were my lungs and vocal chords, so when I had Candida overgrowth for many years I also suffered daily coughs, throat clearing, and phlegm. During my toughest years with Candida I couldn't sing my high notes, as it literally took my singing voice away. Some of my clients will experience recurring bladder or kidney infections, some of them liver problems, sinus infections, migraines, eczema or psoriasis. It really depends on the individual, and where the body's weak area is. The weak spot within the body will usually correlate with an emotional or mental blockage or past trauma that may be from this lifetime, ancestral or from a past life. My lungs and throat used to be my weak spot due to stuck grief and sadness and an inability to express my truth, while shutting down my singing talent due to years and years of sexual and emotional abuse. (Kundalini also showed me various traumatic past life deaths around my throat that needed healing, and of course there was ancestral wounding here to clear out too.)

Toxins cause absolute havoc within the physical body keeping most humans enslaved within a daily fog pushing from their exhausted adrenals to just get through the day.

The point here is that systemic Candida Albicans, parasites and heavy metal toxicity will place a prolonged strain on the physical body where the symptoms will appear within the body's weak area. This is exactly why most practitioners, even some kinesiologists, will miss the link to negative fungal overgrowth, parasites or heavy metal toxicity. These toxins cause absolute havoc within the physical body keeping most humans enslaved within a daily fog pushing from their exhausted adrenals to just get through the day.

The good news is that YOU CAN CHANGE, PURIFY, CLEANSE AND HEAL this!

14

FASTING AND DETOXIFICATION

Detoxing the physical body is an absolute necessity for our awakening process. I frequently experienced spontaneous detoxification that repeated again and again along my personal healing journey. In the early stages of my healing path, I didn't realise what was going on and I just couldn't understand why my body was holding so many toxins. My body was in fact letting go of toxins as I was doing the inner work required for raising my energetic spiritual vibration. I began to use liver and blood cleansing herbs and increased my liquids to assist my body during these phases. When we detoxify the cells in our bodies have a chance to repair and heal.

It is imperative that the body is purified and detoxed from internal parasites, Candida Albicans overgrowth and heavy metal and pesticide/ additive toxicity. Detoxing from the above are so incredibly powerful that it can heal chronic health disorders, mental disorders and other imbalances. Clearing the body from heavy metal toxicity alone can heal addictions! When the body is sufficiently purified from parasites, Candida and heavy metals it will have a healthy PH balance which is essential for optimal health and energy levels. You'll feel clear, sparkly and full of energy when clean and clear of all these toxins.

Fasting alone will not clear out heavy metal, Candida or parasitic toxicity from the physical body! But, it is still a wonderful cleanse for the body giving the cells of the body an opportunity to cleanse and regenerate. Personally, I would first clear out Candida, Parasites and Heavy Metal toxicity before doing weekly or monthly one or two-day fasts to maintain my health. In other words, detox safely from the above first before attempting a healthy one-to-three day fast. Also, always check with your health practitioner first. If you are on medication you'll definitely need to make sure with your doctor whether a fast would be safe for you to undertake.

There are hundreds of different types of fasting methods, so you really need to do what you feel drawn to. For me I felt best on a fast of light soups, smoothies, fresh juices and liver and blood cleansing herbs such as milk thistle, dandelion leaf and root, artichokes and burdock. By supporting my body in this way, I wouldn't suffer headaches, and I'd still be able to meditate alongside the detox. But it is also important to note that my 'normal' day-to-day diet may be seen as a detox diet for others. I do not consume wheat, refined sugar, dairy, meat, alcohol, coffee, tea, soya, beans, pulses or artificial additives. I have been on this diet for nearly 15 years and it has been serving me well. As we continue to raise our vibration we can transcend any diet, such as the blood-group diet. It is my feeling that we need less meat as we keep raising our energetic frequency. My body nowadays craves vegetables, salads, nuts and seeds.

Food Intolerances

More and more people are waking up to the fact that they have food intolerances, and you are only to notice all the 'Free From' food sections in our major supermarkets to see how epidemic this has become. Food intolerances are different to food allergies, as an allergy may be life threatening and a food intolerance reaction can range from sinus backdrop to feeling hungover or depressed. A food allergy can be immediate, whereas a food intolerance can often show up only on the following day. When the gut is compromised due to our unnatural way of living, the gut lining may become porous leaking tiny food particles directly into the bloodstream. The body then becomes riddled with toxins and unwanted by-products from these foods.

You may want to consider avoiding the following foods permanently from your diet, as these seem to be the major culprits concerning food intolerances:

Refined sugar

Refined sugar always produces a weak muscle on everyone I muscle test with Kinesiology, as it is incredibly acidic and literally feeds the bad bacteria in the gut. It is one of the major causes of Candida overgrowth and I have heard of people who have healed themselves from cancers by cutting refined sugar completely from their diets. It is bad for our teeth, bad for our guts and bad for our health. End of.

Alternative solution: I like to use Canadian maple syrup, coconut palm sugar and dates sparingly as a sugar substitute. But, these should not be used when clearing Candida or parasites from the gut, as they're still too acidic when detoxing from negative funguses and parasites.

Wheat

Most of my clients and too many people I know have wheat intolerances. Due to overproduction, genetic modification, toxic pesticides and flour treatment agents we are left with a grain that has become detrimental to the delicate balance of our gut. Wheat retains water in the body, and can negatively affect the sinuses, alongside the gut or of course the body's weak spot. For instance, I've seen children's eczema improve or dramatically clear up by completely giving up wheat. Wheat may also be a cause for depression.

Cow's milk

Cow's milk is actually meant for calves not humans. Cows have four stomachs, and digest milk in a very different way to humans. It is true that some human beings can tolerate it in small amounts, but from my experience as a Kinesiologist, I've seen it test negative on too many clients to ever consider drinking it again. It is mucus forming and acidic for the body. I always find it laughable when I read in a so-called health or mother's magazine how a glass of milk can relieve indigestion! This couldn't be further from the truth. It may feel like it is relieving it in the immediate moment, but it is actually causing it in the long run.

Coffee

Coffee is yet another substance that often comes up to avoid for my clients. It is a stimulant and highly toxic to our body's natural health and balance. Often clients who are severely adrenally fatigued will be living off the stimulating energy that coffee offers, and feel they are unable to give it up as they need the extra energy. Usually we have to detox the body from toxicity first, and then we begin to heal the adrenals with herbs and vitamins so that we can feel our own energy from within and capitalise upon our bodies natural rhythms rather than pushing upstream against our natural flow.

Solution: I love making my own almond milk and to heat it slightly with barley and chicory as a coffee alternative. With homemade almond milk you can use a whisk to froth it up and make yourself a restaurant quality latte or hot drink. Another alternative is to use matcha green tea powder instead of coffee. You can use this powder to make a hot drink with almond milk and it has a natural slow release energising effect on the body. You'll only need a half to one teaspoon per day as it has a stimulating effect on the body but it is far healthier than coffee of course.

Raw cacao can also give you a more natural boost, either eating it raw, or making a hot chocolate using hemp, almond or other alternative and preferably homemade milks.

Food intolerances have a nasty habit of only showing up a day later with symptoms that can range from nasal backdrop, indigestion to depression, a hungover feeling, or even anxiety.

Soya

Soya is an oestrogen stimulant and most of the soya in our world is unfortunately genetically modified. It seems to have a negative effect on our delicate endocrine or hormonal system and often tests negative on my clients.

E-additives

Artificial food additives also test negative on ALL of my clients. They're generally highly toxic and negatively disrupt the endocrine.

Pre- and Post-Fasting

Three days leading up to your fast and three days after your fast is an important time to assist your gut in preparation and readjusting. In fact, if you do eat wheat, dairy, meat and refined sugar, I would cut these out a few weeks before undertaking any liquid fast. Also, if you suspect you have Candida or parasitic toxicity then I would go to see a professional and experienced Nutritionist or Kinesiologist to assist you in the process of safely detoxing from these first. A normal juice fast or even colonics and enemas will not remove systemic Candida or parasitic toxicity from the whole body.

(When you look for a practitioner to work with regarding Candida, parasites and heavy metals, ask for testimonials, and talk to the practitioner first to see if they truly understand the process of detoxification. Unfortunately, there aren't many health practitioners who are experienced in this field, but if you persist you will be able to find the right practitioner to work with.)

During these 3 days of pre- and post-fast make sure to keep your diet incredibly pure, by only eating fresh vegetables and fruits with pure spring water, lemon, olive oil and apple cider vinegar.

Variations of fasts that may inspire you

Lemon in water

At my son's school science fair recently there was a boy who had done his project using various different solutions to clean a dirty two pence coin. There were at least 6 or 7 different solutions including strong chemicals and also vinegar. I asked him which solution cleaned the coin the fastest and most effectively. Of course, it was lemon and salt!

Lemons are incredibly cleansing and I use them daily on almost everything. Even though they're acidic, they have an alkalising effect on the physical body.

I would often start even my non-fasting days by squirting a few lemons into two litres of pure spring water. I would then make sure to drink all of it before lunch. You can however do a lemon and water fast for a few days to clear out the body from toxicity. This type of fast may cause headaches and discomfort, so make sure not to work and to rest instead. Your body will need extra sleep as your cells repair during the fast.

To avoid negative symptoms like headaches when fasting consider drinking Milk Thistle, Dandelion leaf, Dandelion Root, Artichoke or Burdock. These herbs/foods will assist your liver with clearing all the excess toxins from the body.

A note on Salt

There is good salt and bad salt. Bad salt is refined table salt. Good salts are usually grey unrefined salts, such as Celtic sea salt. These salts are very good for the body as they are high in mineral content and trace elements, such as calcium, magnesium, copper, iron and potassium. I find when my body is not getting enough salt I tend to get foot and leg cramps. A dose of good salts always heals this issue within minutes.

Soups

Here you can choose to have a thin or a thick soup. I would make the soup with organic vegetables and then liquidise it before drinking it as a meal. On this type of fast you'll still feel sustained and may be able to carry on working, although it is always preferable to rest as much as possible during a fast. You may want to consider a 1- or 2-day soup fast when the weather is cold.

Juicing

You may feel inspired to juice for two or three days. This way you will still get all of your vitamins and minerals while cleansing out your colon. Raw vegetables and fruit juice are full of enzymes, minerals and vitamins. You can virtually juice any vegetable or fruit, so get creative and enjoy the process.

The clean and centred feeling you get once your fast is completed is truly wonderful. I'd often feel brand new and refreshed with boundless energy. It definitely makes the uncomfortable symptoms of fasting worthwhile!

Feel free to do a 1-day, 2-day or even 3-day fast. Personally, I wouldn't do more than 7 days, and even 7 days I wouldn't do on my own – there are many retreat centres worldwide that offer safe 7- or 10-day fasts.

You may also feel drawn to implement a fast in your weekly routine by doing a one-day fast weekly, or a weekend fast monthly to keep your body clean and clear of toxicity.

A note on Flax Seeds

Eating two to three tablespoons of flax seeds daily can heal chronic constipation. Constipation is always a sign of toxicity, and flax seeds will help to move the toxins out of the body via the small and large intestine. Even though we excrete toxins through our urine and sweat, we actually excrete most of our body's toxins through the bowels so it is very important to keep the bowels moving daily, preferably twice daily.

15

DETOXING FROM HEAVY METALS

Heavy metals such as mercury, aluminium, cadmium, arsenic, lead, uranium, and foods that have been contaminated by being canned in aluminium; vegetables sprayed by pesticides; fish or vaccines filled with mercury; old paint coverings and plumbing; industrial waste pollutants and other pollutants in our air and water can build up inside the physical body causing neurological disorders, degenerative, chronic and lowered or auto-immunity, impotence and addictions. I treated a young boy with autism recently and we needed to clear Candida overgrowth and also heavy metals from his body. Once we healed his gut and cleared his body from heavy metal toxicity his daily emotional outbursts came to an end.

Clearing your body from heavy metal toxicity may be so powerful for you that it will bring you to LIFE by transforming you deeply from the inside out benefiting you in ways you may never even have imagined!

If you do have amalgam fillings I'd begin the process of replacing these with white or even gold fillings. Go to a dentist who'll use a rubber dam to place inside your mouth while extracting the amalgams so that you won't risk any of the mercury leeching back into your body. Removing amalgam fillings will not clear the body from mercury toxicity though. After removing these fillings you'll need to actively detox the physical body from mercury toxicity.

Heavy Metal Toxicity will cause an imbalance of chemicals, such as dopamine in your brain. When there is an imbalance in the brain chemicals we are more prone to addictive behaviours, impaired sleeping patterns, sexual dysfunctions such as low sex drive in men and women, infertility, erectile dysfunction and premature ejaculation in men, etc, and other mental instabilities and neurological disorders such as Alzheimer's. Clearing your body from heavy metal toxicity may be so powerful for you that it will bring you to LIFE by transforming you deeply from the inside out benefiting you in ways you may never even have imagined! You have nothing to lose so you may as well give it a go.

How to clear the body naturally from heavy metal toxicity

Zeolite liquid
Although controversial even among Natural Health Practitioners, this is my personal favourite as it was brought to me in a divine and synchronistic way a few weeks before my Kundalini awakening. One of my friends brought me a bottle of dark liquid zeolite and told me to give it a go as she was given many bottles for her son who had cancer at the time. I put it to one side thinking I'd look it up later. In the meantime, my oldest son who was 3 at the time asked me if he could see an actual volcano. We browsed on YouTube and watched videos of volcanos, and in particular we really enjoyed watching the videos where the lava would hit the ocean, as it was incredibly dramatic and spectacular. Right after watching these videos he jumped off my lap to go and play in his room and I decided to look up zeolite. Amazed yet again at the beauty of synchronicity and magic I discovered that zeolite was a compound that was created when lava hit the ocean! I immediately started working with liquid Zeolite and cleared the heavy metal build up within my physical body. There are meant to be no side effects except for feeling thirstier than usual, but due to my sensitivity I did really feel the detox and couldn't take as many drops as suggested on the bottle!

Two weeks after working with zeolite I experienced a powerful spiritual awakening,

Tip 1: Combine this detox with Milk Thistle, Dandelion root and leaf, artichoke and similar liver and blood cleansing herbs to assist your body in the detoxification process.

Tip 2: Ground-up linseeds, also known as flax seeds, will help to clean out the bowel and also assist in the process of detoxification. You can take up to three tablespoons per day with extra water for best results.

Tip 3: I've always used zeolites in combination with high doses of chlorella.

Cilantro (coriander)

I love coriander and have always found it to be very cleansing and refreshing. I was delighted to hear that it also clears out heavy metals from the body. Of course, we would have to eat it in high doses, so you could make a pesto with coriander, pine nuts and garlic mixed in with olive oil and lemon to pull out toxins naturally from the body. YUM!

Tip: I would use cilantro pesto in combination with zeolite and chlorella for optimal results.

Chlorella

Chlorella is high in chlorophyll and appears to bind to heavy metals to remove them safely from the physical body. I love combining it with zeolite when I detox from heavy metals.

Burdock root

Burdock root removes metals such as mercury along with other toxins like Candida and parasitic toxicity. It is a great blood and liver cleanser and works well in combination with dandelion root and leaf, and milk thistle. This is also one of my go-to herbs for clearing Candida and parasitic toxicity.

Bentonite Clay

Bentonite Clay is a form of volcanic ash and has the ability to remove impurities and heavy metal toxicity when used safely in the correct way. Please seek the advice of a health practitioner in order to use it safely.

MSM (Methylsulfonymethane)

It is a naturally occurring substance found in fresh raw foods grown on the natural rain cycle and is incredibly effective at detoxifying your body!

NAC

NAC (N-Acetyl-Cysteine), is a natural sulfur-containing amino acid derived from natural foods. It is also a powerful anti-oxidant and can repair oxidative damage in the physical body. It is particularly good for detoxing from mercury or amalgam fillings, cadmium (from cigarette smoke) and lead from paint. NAC chelates heavy metals and slowly pulls them out of the body.

Nettles

Yes, you've read it correctly. Stinging nettles from your garden can help you detox from heavy metals and other toxins keeping the liver and kidneys clean. Nettles are a superfood and can also help to keep the adrenals healed and balanced while strengthening bones within the body. I recently read of a woman who was diagnosed with premature osteoporosis many years ago, and who then started to drink Nettle infusions twice a week. Many years on she was retested and her bones were healthier than most 20 year olds! All the more reason to dose up on Nettles!

EDTA

EDTA (Ethylenediamine tetraacetic acid) is a polyprotic acid contain four carboxylic acid groups and two amine groups with lone-pair electrons that chelate calcium and several other metal ions.[1] It is specifically good for detoxing the body from lead, but must be used only via medical supervision.

---

[1] Source: www.ncbi.nlm.nih.gov/pubmed/17484616

Glutathione
Glutathione is derived from fresh fruits and vegetables and helps to remove toxins from cigarette smoke, auto exhaust, lead, mercury and deadly PCB's. Glutathione can also remove old toxic build up from alcohol in the liver. I have read somewhere that children who have autism can be deficient in Glutathione. It can also be incredibly helpful for people who suffer with autoimmune diseases to supplement with Glutathione.

R-Lipoic Acid
Another powerful anti-oxidant that detoxes the body from heavy metals. It works well in combination with EDTA and can be referred to as Quick Silver.

Garlic
Taking garlic capsules and also eating it raw is an incredibly safe way to pull toxins such as lead from the body.

Detox foot patches
Using detoxification foot patches can be incredibly helpful during any fast or detox. It is a very safe and in my experience, effective way of detoxing the body at night while we're sleeping.

Implementing new and improved lifestyle changes to prevent heavy metal toxicity
Once you have detoxed your body from heavy metals, and you feel the incredible health benefits including increased energy and overall wellness, you may well be motivated to permanently cut out products that may cause recontamination.

These include avoiding or cutting down on:
- PBA's in plastic.
- Non-organic vegetables, fruits and salads contaminated with pesticides that contain heavy metals.
- Farmed fish, especially tuna and salmon that is well-known for containing high levels of mercury.
- Please do consider removing all amalgam fillings.
- Conventional shampoos, conditioners and other skin

products and perfumes.
- Make up. Apparently, there are high levels of lead in 60% of conventional lipstick!

In extreme cases, you may want to move house to get away from old pipes contaminated by lead, paints, carpets, etc.

16

CANDIDA ALBICANS

What is it?

Candida Albicans is a yeast or fungus that lives within the large intestine, and, in a healthy person, this is where it remains in perfect balance with good bacteria. When the immune system becomes compromised and the number of beneficial bacteria declines, Candida starts to multiply and disseminates to other organs causing polystemic Candidiasis.

Causes

An overgrowth of Candida Albicans is thought to effect around one third of the population in the West (personally, I feel it effects way more people), due to the clinical overuse of antibiotics, which is widely recognised as a major cause. Other causes that seem to exert a similar effect are the oral contraceptive, HRT, steroids, such as corticosteroids, an acidic diet (think sugar) and stress.

Candida and Kinesiology

As every single person is biochemically different, everyone will display different symptoms, and would also need a uniquely tailored treatment plan. This is why I believe Applied Kinesiology is one of the best healing modalities for the treatment of Candida overgrowth. With muscle testing and the right combinations of herbs and nutrition it is easy to determine not only if someone has Candida overgrowth, but also what level they have it at, and how it can be treated for that specific person's needs. Information is taken from the body via muscle testing, and then relayed to the practitioner who will then be able to determine what it is the person needs.

Candida sufferers usually display a different variety of food intolerances or chemical sensitivities unique to them.

To devise a standard treatment plan for everyone with Candida overgrowth is to miss the point completely. One set treatment will not be a cure for all sufferers of Candida! Clearing Candida is a lengthy process that must be understood by the practitioner for it to be successfully undertaken by the client. Recommending caprylic acid for all clients, which some practitioners do, is simply not good enough for people who have severe cases of polystemic Candidiasis. Following a set Candida diet is also to misunderstand this process of detoxification and elimination. When I suffered severe Candida overgrowth myself I could not tolerate soya, beans or pulses, and yet I was eating these foods daily thinking my diet was impeccable as I'd cut out wheat, sugar and cow's milk. Everyone is different, and responds differently to foods, environment, emotional issues, etc. It is also important to eat fruit, and the standard Candida diet will tell you to avoid all fruits. I didn't eat fruit for two years, and when I finally started healing with the help of my Kinesiologist, I was incredibly relieved to be able to eat fruit again. Fruit is after all incredibly cleansing and the FOS (fructose) feeds the good bacteria in the gut too!

One of the first things I do when I see a client who shows high levels of Candida is to tailor a detox program to support the body in eliminating excess toxins. Usually clients with high levels of Candida will have high levels of toxins in the body, and these toxins are causing extreme fatigue, constipation or irritable bowel, depression, and other uncomfortable symptoms. Once enough toxins have been removed from the body, by avoiding foods that would place stress on the body and by taking detoxifying herbs/remedies, I would test for herbs or a remedy that would target to clear the Candida overgrowth. While clearing the Candida, the detoxifying herbs would have to be taken alongside the cleansing herbs so as to avoid uncomfortable 'die off' symptoms. Candida 'die off' symptoms are well known amongst Candida sufferers and experts. When Candida is killed off, the cells split and create more toxins, and this is why it is important to clear the body of toxic overload first, and then to continue detoxifying the body alongside clearing the Candida with anti-fungal herbs, flower remedies or foods. Once the Candida is cleared the gut needs to be healed and repopulated with good bacteria. At this stage I would also look at emotional issues related to the imbalance that would need to be addressed to avoid a return. Dietary changes may change again once the body is stronger.

Candida overgrowth is waking us up from our toxic lifestyles, and to help us reassess how we relate to life emotionally, physically, spiritually and mentally. How much can the body take? Yes, we are resilient, and the body has an amazing capability to heal itself, but we live in an unnatural world filled with toxic diets, drugs, environment, electromagnetic stress, and then not to even mention the stressful relationships we have in our personal or professional lives.

I still find muscle testing nothing short of miraculous. Your body knows what is good for you. Trust that!

When healing the gut, it is very important to also heal our boundaries, our self-esteem and to step deeply into our spiritual power.

Candida and Emotions

Funguses tend to emotionally correspond with low self-esteem and disempowerment. Whereas *parasites* tend to display as a lack of boundaries. Funguses and parasites tend to work together as they both thrive in acidic environments. Low self-esteem and diminished boundaries also tend to work together. When healing the gut, it is very important to also heal our boundaries, our self-esteem and to step deeply into our spiritual power.

Cleansing the body from Candida toxicity

1. **Herbs** such as Milk Thistle, Red Clover, Burdock, Dandelion leaf, Dandelion root and artichoke will support your body to safely let go of toxicity. How much you need

to drink or take daily depends on how severe your case of Candida overgrowth is. This is why it is incredibly helpful to have an experienced practitioner to assist you in this process.

2. **Avoiding all sugars accept for whole fresh fruits. The** best fruits to keep eating are apples, berries, pomegranates and melons. (I would still avoid bananas, mangoes and pineapples, as these fruits tend to be very sweet and acidic)

3. **Avoiding wheat, dairy, soya, coffee, tea, alcohol,** or any other foods you may feel are irritating your gut. It really does vary from person to person. As Hippocrates said, "one man's meat is another man's poison".

4. You'll need to **remove all toxic cleaning products, clothes' washing powders, shampoos, conditioners and body washes** and replacing with natural ones. Indian soap pods are a fantastic alternative to clothes' washing powder. 'Green People' products here in the UK seem to test well on all of my clients too.

After one month of doing the four steps above you can add in your anti-fungal herbs or oxygen powder and barley grass powders to actually kill off the Candida. In some cases, you'd do this for two months, and for others, four months. It really depends on how severe the overgrowth is. It is important to carry on with the four steps above while killing off the negative funguses in the body.

Anti-fungal herbs (start with a small dose and increase dosage slowly to avoid 'die off' symptoms)

- Oregano oil capsules
- black pepper
- turmeric
- goldenseal
- pomegranate
- Barley grass powder
- Oxygen powder or drops
- Pau d'Arco, also known as Lapacho
- Black walnut

- Neem
- Olive Leaf Extract
- Garlic
- Tea tree
- Calendula
- Green Essence, Spinifex, Bottlebrush and Peach-flowered Tea-tree from Australian Bush for infants, children and animals

Clearing Candida in children and animals

When I treat infants and children in my clinic, I mainly use flower remedies alongside an elimination diet. Babies and children have a pure vibration and so respond well to flower remedies.

Green Essence from Australian Bush Flower Essences is the essence to have in your medicine cupboard if you have children. They'll need to avoid sugar, and often wheat and cow's milk, while taking 5 drops of Green Essences, 5 minutes before meals, 3 times per day. There is a 6-week program children can follow to cleanse from candida overgrowth.

Australian Bush Flower Essences Candida Cleanse Protocol for infants, children & animals

- **Week 1 and 2** *Green Essences* 5 drops 5 mins before meals, 3 times per day; *Peach-Flowered Tea-Tree* 7 drops, morning and night.
- **Week 3 and 4** *Spinifex, Peach-Flowered Tea-Tree* and *Bottlebrush*, 7 drops morning and night. (mix all three in same bottle).
- **Week 5 and 6** *Peach-Flowered Tea-Tree*, 7 drops morning and night.

Once you've ordered your master or stock bottles you can make up your own remedy using a 20ml or 30ml empty dropper bottle. Use a tiny amount of brandy mixed with water to preserve remedy while adding 7 drops from your stock bottle. For infants, you can use water only, but then the mixture needs to live in the fridge and must be consumed within 2 weeks.

17

PARASITES

There are hundreds of different variations of parasites that love to cause toxins, stress and acidity within the physical body. Parasites can be very tricky to clear and again it is best to see an experienced practitioner who can assist you alongside also looking at funguses and diet. Parasitic toxicity, like Candida toxicity, is highly toxic and may cause extreme fatigue, bloating, abdominal pain, irritability and other nasty symptoms. As I've mentioned before, parasites tend to go hand in hand with a lack of boundaries and self-worth, so it is very important to begin to heal emotionally alongside your parasitic detox. Practice saying no, go away, this is not for me!

There are various different ways to detox from parasite toxicity while killing off the parasites and their eggs.

Black walnut, garlic, oregano oil, clove, ginger and wormwood are commonly used herbs to help clear out parasites from the body.

It is also important to starve parasites by avoiding sugar, so often parasites tend to go as we heal the body of Candida overgrowth. But in some cases, parasites are the priority cleanse. It really depends on the individual case.

Make sure, that as you cleanse, you give a chance for the eggs that the parasites lay to also be killed off. This is why some people will cleanse the body for two weeks, then take two weeks off and then cleanse the body again for a further two weeks.

As we're all bio-chemically individual and different there is no clear-cut standard recipe for everyone to follow.

Special Note

I highly recommend you work with *Purifying Essence* from the Australian Bush Flower Combination Essences. I've been working with this combination essence on and off for 15 years. It has helped me clear out built-up emotional baggage and by-products alongside all of my fasts and detoxes. It may be a vibrational essence, but for me I feel its effects very powerfully in my physical body. Within hours I get clearer in my field when I work with it during a detox. I really cannot recommend it highly enough!

18

ELECTROMAGNETIC STRESS/POLLUTION

Televisions, hairdryers, microwaves, mobile/cell phones, Wifi, smart meters, etc all cause artificial electronic waves that disrupt our natural energy systems and bodies. When the immune system is functioning well we are strong enough to withstand its negative effects, but when the body's immune system becomes compromised we can begin to feel the serious negative effects of electro smog. This is why most of my clients who suffer from auto-immune system disorders tend to be severely negatively affected by electromagnetic pollution.

There are various different solutions to this issue, and again, I would use kinesiology to find out what would be the priority action to take for each individual client. Here's just a few that may be of interest:

- **Orgonite, dark or clear quartz crystals** may be helpful here.
- **Electro Essence** from Australian Bush Flower Essences can be used daily to dispel the negative effects of electro smog.
- **Earthing sheets** may help.
- There are various **wall units** that are usually plugged into the wall specifically designed to protect the body from electro smog/waves.

- The **crystal shungite** can also be worn to help protect against electro smog.
- Do consider **turning off your router and mobile phones** at night.

19

AUTO-IMMUNE DISORDERS

Auto-immunity is on the rise, and in my opinion, is a direct result of our unnatural toxic world. The body gets very confused and begins to act out of balance. Self-hatred and attack or self-sabotage can also often be linked emotionally to auto-immunity, as the cells in the body begin to attack themselves.

I also suspect that energetic implants and artificial intelligence implanted by negative astral beings may be a major cause for Auto-immune Disorders. Of course, in our 3D reality system we aren't yet able to see or detect these devices within the physical body, so it seems as if the body is attacking itself, when the body is in fact attacking a foreign entity or implant within the body.

To heal auto-immunity I'd look at clearing the gut from heavy metal, Candida and parasite toxicity, sticking to a healthy balanced plant-based diet and doing deep emotional and mental body clearing work while teaching my client to deeply love themselves by expressing their boundaries to those around them. Of course, this is again a process that will take time and patience, but if you are committed you can heal.

I would also consider spending more time in nature alongside positive visualisation, and positive thinking. Of course, we do not want to go into denial by only focussing on the positive, but we certainly do not want to throw the baby out with the bathwater. Positive thinking can most definitely assist us in healing our physical, mental, emotional and spiritual bodies. As long as we stay focussed on solutions, rather than dwelling on the problem, we then allow for energy to shift and change internally. If we are stuck in a negative thinking loop things will never change for us. It is therefore imperative that we make the effort to change the way we think when we heal our physical body. This is why EFT, meditation and prayer can be so incredibly effective, as it is changing old negative belief patterns from the body/mind and exchanging these for positive new ones enabling for us to change our daily reality for the better.

20

HEALING THE HORMONAL SYSTEM

Our body's delicate hormonal system will get thrown off balance with Candida overgrowth, parasites, heavy metal toxicity, stress, sexual wounding, over working or/and not resting enough. Often clearing the gut from heavy metal toxicity, Candida and parasitic toxicity and overgrowth, will have an automatic healing and balancing effect on the endocrine. It is thus incredibly important to treat the gut alongside treating the body's hormones.

Eating artificial GMO foods and drinking tap water that has been contaminated with fluoride and the birth control pill hormones, or eating un-organic chicken and meat where the animals are injected with hormones will also impact your endocrine in a negative way. When the endocrine or body's hormones are out of balance we may feel ungrounded, put on or lose weight, feel depressed or anxious, suffer from addiction, feel so stressed that the tiniest upset will cause great distress (adrenal fatigue), have thyroid or ovarian/testes dysfunction and other unpleasant symptoms.

Healing the Pineal

When the pineal gland is out of balance we may not be sleeping very well. A quick and simple balance for the pineal is to shine a red laser beam that you can find on the back of certain writing pens, directly at the area between your eyebrows with your eyes shut for a few minutes (ensuring you don't look at the red light). When the Pineal gland is in balance we will usually experience restful and reparative sleep. The Pineal also corresponds with your intuitive or psychic perception or third eye chakra. Some people believe it is the seat of the soul. When we meditate we are also balancing this gland.

Healing the Thyroid

The thyroid is a gland that is shaped a bit like a bow tie or a butterfly and is located at the base of the neck in between the clavicles. It produces a hormone called thyroxin which helps to regulate metabolism, heart rate, and in children, their growth and development. Imbalances can be either an under-functioning or over-functioning thyroid. To keep the thyroid balanced we need to rest, have a healthy diet, exercise and reduce stress in our day-to-day lives. The thyroid also links in with the throat chakra and expression. When we are in victim consciousness and shut down, unable to express our truth, or in a relationship where we allow for someone else to overpower us, we may begin to experience thyroid dysfunction. It is therefore very important to do healing work around the throat chakra to also assist the thyroid to heal. We may need to leave a relationship where we are not permitted to shine in our power and express our truth. Iodine is the king of natural supplements that may have a healing and balancing effect on the thyroid, but needs to be taken with care, especially if you are on thyroid medication. If you want to try this supplement and if you are on thyroxin, ask your doctor and health practitioner to work together in assisting you to slowly come off your medication. Eating a raw food diet may also have an incredibly healing effect on the thyroid, as I have heard of people healing their thyroid disorders by going 100% raw.

A simple daily energetic balancing self-help tool

We place three fingers in the soft spot in between the clavicles and three fingers on one of our temples. We allow our fingers to softly rest here for a few minutes until we have a yawn, burp, sigh or tummy gurgle. We then place three fingers again in the soft spot in between the clavicles and on the opposite temple for a similar amount of time.

If you are experiencing thyroid issues I would highly recommend using this technique daily to assist in the healing of this gland.

You may also want to consider learning how to communicate with Non-Violent Communication techniques. You can google to see if there are any workshops or courses in your area, or research books that have been written about this powerful yet simple way of communication. I do elaborate on this technique further a little later on in this book (page 222).

Figure 8: A Simple Daily Energetic Balance

Hold with three fingers of one hand (index, middle and ring) lightly on one temple, and three fingers of the other hand in the soft spot in between the clavicles, above the sternum.

Hold these points together for a few minutes, then switch hands to hold the other temple and again the soft spot.

Healing the immune system (Thymus)

The thymus gland, a triangular organ located near the heart and the thyroid, is associated with immunity, and creates T-cells that are an incredibly important type of white blood cells and that help the body fight off viruses, bacteria and disease. This gland tends to shrink after puberty, but it is my feeling that we can strengthen this gland and for it to even grow strong again as we heal our self-esteem. When we are strong in ourselves with self-love and boundaries, we are also protected from those who may want to cause us harm.

> *When we are strong in ourselves with self-love and boundaries, we are also protected from those who may want to cause us harm.*

Deep tissue or lymphatic massage is incredibly healing for our physical and also emotional, mental and spiritual bodies. When our lymphatic system gets blocked up and stagnant it will have a negative effect on the rest of our bodies, and when we're feeling blocked spiritually, mentally or emotionally it may represent as blocked lymphatic points within the physical body. You are therefore giving yourself a great service by receiving deep tissue massage as frequently as you can.

Yoga can have a similar effect to massage, so if you're saving your pennies get out your yoga mat and do some daily stretches to get your lymphatic system in flow. Or enjoy a jump on the trampoline with the kids.

Thymus thump

Tapping the thymus, which is roughly located next to your sternum, to the left and slightly below the soft spot in between the clavicles, can send out a reminder for the thymus to do its job. Tapping in three's, to the rhythm of a waltz while making an affirmation around loving oneself can really strengthen this gland and your immune system.

Candida, Parasites and the Immune System

Candida and parasites will lower the body's immunity, so usually as we clear these from the gut and the rest of the body; we also need to support the immune system with high doses of Vitamin C and Zinc. It is perfectly safe to take Vitamin C in large doses to support your immunity, and there have been cases reported where people have cured various degenerative diseases with large doses of Vitamin C alone.

Once an overgrowth of Candida is cleared from the gut the body's immune system will begin to heal and function normally again. Although I've experienced that in really chronic and severe cases of Candida that the person may also need to supplement with herbs to strengthen immunity more long term. I had to do this after I initially healed from Candida overgrowth in my own gut. It took me 9 months to heal my immune system with the support of herbs, vitamin C and zinc.

Exercise and Immunity

When our bodies are strong and we're exercising frequently, our immune systems tend to benefit tremendously, so it is important to strengthen our physical bodies. Also, a strong physical body often corresponds with a good self-esteem, and it would be very difficult for entities or energetic parasites to latch on to your energetic field or physical body when you're fit and grounded. Staying physically fit and strong strengthens us emotionally, spiritually and mentally. But don't exercise if you're suffering adrenal burnout or fatigue. It is very important to heal the body first, and then to strengthen with exercise afterwards.

Healing and balancing the Adrenals

The adrenals are two small glands that sit right on top of the kidneys that produces a few different hormones including adrenalin, a hormone we need during times of stress. Many people these days suffer from adrenal fatigue. Adrenal fatigue often goes hand-in-hand with Candida or parasitic overgrowth. When we work too hard, running and rushing from one thing to another we are not giving our bodies a chance to rest and repair. As we may thrive or even be driven by stress our adrenals will suffer the consequences. One of the signs of adrenal fatigue is tiredness even when we wake in the morning, and also not being able to handle the little things in life, and when everything begins to feel insurmountable. To heal the adrenals, we must heal the gut as stress can cause Candida overgrowth due to acidifying the body, and alongside this process of healing we need to supplement with adrenal herbs, large doses of Vitamin C (at least 3000mg per day) and Multi B complex around three times per day, and most importantly we need to take time out to rest. Taking an adrenal supplement may be necessary in some more extreme cases, and supplementing with B3 or B5 on top of your Multi B Complex may also be helpful in some cases. Drinking Nettle infusions daily may also assist us in repairing our adrenals. Do consider avoiding coffee, sugar and cocoa (chocolate) from your diet when repairing the adrenals. We need to teach our adrenals how to relax so that we can find our natural energy from within ourselves rather than being reliant on stimulants outside of ourselves for energy.

When we work too hard, running and rushing from one thing to another we are not giving our bodies a chance to rest and repair. As we may thrive or even be driven by stress our adrenals will suffer the consequences.

21

REPRODUCTIVE HEALTH

Ovarian Health

To keep the ovaries healthy, we need to make sure our body is mainly alkaline and clean from toxicity. Coffee and soya is well known for having a negative effect on ovaries so cut these from your diet permanently if you're having issues regarding your ovaries. You can clear acidity from the body by clearing Candida and parasitic toxicity, while incorporating ginger and turmeric into your diet. Ginger has been shown to kill ovarian cancer cells! You can grate ginger into all of your salad dressings and make a health drink with hot water, fresh ginger slices and lemon in it. Placing castor oil pack on your lower abdomen may also reduce any inflammation from the ovaries.

Emotionally you will need to go inwards to root out any sexual trauma memories, and to clear these with EFT, ESR and flower essences. It is important to teach and show your unconscious mind that the trauma is over and that you are safe now. You can also speak directly to your ovaries with love and forgiveness for what may have happened in the past.

There is a link between the throat and the sacral (sexual/creative) chakra, as children who were abused sexually will often shut down their voice out of shame, guilt or to protect the abuser. They also shut down their voice due to the cultural or religious mask we are taught to wear to always be nice to everyone, due to feelings of unworthiness, shame and guilt. As we heal our sexual wounding it is important to create a safe healing space where we can go back into the memory and express our boundaries claiming back our power.

We need to unfreeze the abused child within if we really want to let the trauma go and to move forward more freely. We also need to practice saying no, whilst asserting our boundaries with people in our day-to-day lives.

You can speak directly to your ovaries with love and forgiveness for what may have happened in the past.

If we are unable to conceive children due to an ovarian imbalance you may want to ask the question how it serves you not having children. You may be blocking your desire with unconscious fears around parenthood, childbirth, or the responsibility of raising children.

Wisteria and *She Oak* in the Australian Bush Flower Essence range may help to dislodge old unconscious limiting beliefs and patterns that may be holding you back from having healthy ovaries and a healthy sexuality.

Healing the Testes

Saw Palmetto is a wonderful herb that may heal and balance the testes and bring overall wellness to the physical body. It is important to note though to keep the body pure and toxin free, and I have heard of cases where men have totally healed testicular cancer by only eating raw foods. Keeping the body free from heavy metal, Candida and parasitic toxicity will assist in keeping the testes healthy. If you do find yourself with an imbalance here, you can ask the question how it serves for you to have the imbalance. It is also very important to do emotional and mental body healing work around sexual wounding and traumas.

22

THE ENERGETIC BODY, THE AURA & THE CHAKRA SYSTEM

Often when there has been a shock or trauma it can throw our energetic body, the aura and chakra system out of balance. There are various ways we can balance our bodies' chakras and aura but the simplest is using crystals while holding one's hands over each chakra point a few centimetres away from the body while feeling into each point allowing the energy to balance. This is an intuitive practice that will take a bit of time and patience to master. To expand and repair the aura, especially if there was a physical accident, we brush or massage the aura around the body outwards to create a large auric field.

It does happen sometimes where I lock in a past trauma for a client and once we've done the whole healing with stress release and EFT and remedies that I also need to balance the chakras and the aura. This does not happen very often though, but if you do feel that it was a severe trauma and that you need a chakra and aura balance you can do it for yourself by placing various types of crystals on each chakra and dabbing your hands with Rescue Remedy and massaging your own aura. You can use gemstones that correspond with the same colours of the chakra. A red stone for your base chakra, an orange stone like citrine for your sacral chakra, a yellow stone for your solar plexus chakra, a green or pink stone for the heart chakra, a light blue stone for the throat, dark blue for your third eye and purple or clear quartz stone for your crown chakra. Place the stones on the chakra points while lying down on your back. You can play some soft healing music. According to kinesiology-testing, baroque music, like Mozart's symphonies have an incredibly healing effect on the energetic and physical bodies. You can always play this music softly while soaking in the healing balance from the crystals. This process shouldn't take longer than five minutes, but it may feel really good, and you may want to meditate here for a bit longer as you charge up your energetic field.

23

DETOXING FROM MEDIA

One of the best decisions I ever made was to get rid of my TV. That was many years ago now, and I've never looked back since. I felt an immediate improvement in my energy, and I became more capable of actually finishing projects, rather than just starting them. Social media, the Internet, TV, Hollywood, Gossip Magazines etc can all be seen as distractions and ways to unconsciously program the masses on how to behave, what to think, how to feel etc. It is UNNATURAL and FAKE, but as most people still feel unworthy of love and in victim consciousness and even addicted to fear and drama they all jump on the media express train that can only ever lead to inner disassociation, disharmony and confusion. It takes us away from our authentic selves, our connection to nature, to our hearts, our higher selves and God/Goddess. It is the opposite of stillness and presence where we can truly connect with others and ourselves.

> *Social media, the Internet, TV, Hollywood, Gossip Magazines etc can all be seen as distractions and ways to unconsciously program the masses on how to behave, what to think, how to feel.*

Facebook and other forms of social media can become incredibly addictive. If you are feeling stuck with an Internet addiction sign yourself up for a silent retreat and go cold turkey. It will be the sweetest medicine for your soul, and you'll return able to really clear out the habit.

Part IV

HEALING THE MENTAL AND EMOTIONAL BODIES

Often when we purify our mental body we also purify our emotional body, and vice versa. In fact, all of the bodies – the physical, spiritual bodies included – work together in unison as we purify on all levels. EFT for instance clears out mental blockages, but more often than not my client will also be clearing out stuck and trapped emotions as they change their mental patterning or clear out old trauma. Tapping specific EFT points while making our affirmation may suddenly bring about an eruption of grief, rage or emotional pain. It is always a good sign in healing when this happens. Breathwork tends to mainly only work on the emotional body, and what I love about it is that we can keep the mind totally out of the practice and trust the breath to assist us in our emotional releases. Then again both EFT and Breathwork will also have a healing and balancing effect on the physical body. Often mental and emotional blockages will cause dis-ease in the physical body, and in our search for healing our physical bodies, we may find we're guided to healing emotional and mental blockages so that we can heal physically. I've experienced this many times in my own life, and also have seen this happen again and again in my Kinesiology practice.

I had a client who presented with brain damage a few years ago. She had been in a motorbike accident three years before our session and was unable to work due to migraines, crawling sensations in her brain and physical exhaustion. We looked at how it served her to have the accident and the brain damage. She said it was the only thing that would have stopped her at the time, as she was a workaholic before the accident. I assisted her during the session to begin the process of self-love, self-care and placing healthy boundaries. I helped her understand that she now had the lesson of needing to rest, self-care and slowing down without having to stay brain damaged. We used EFT, Bush Flower Remedies and Kinesiology during the session. A few days later she told me that the worst of her symptoms had miraculously healed since our session and that she was now able to work again. There were no supplements involved in her session, and it was ALL done with energetic healing techniques. This is a wonderful example of how healing our mental body can also heal our physical body.

24

HEALING VIA OUR
RELATIONSHIPS

Your relationships with others will reflect where you are in consciousness along your path of awakening. This is why we tend to shift many relationships as we move from unconsciousness to consciousness. It is only natural to let go of the old disempowering relationships as we step deeper and deeper into our own spiritual empowerment. If, for instance, you were entangled in a relationship (not necessarily romantic), where you were being manipulated and subtly controlled and you've done work on your boundaries there will come a time when you'll have to say no to that person. People who do manipulate and control may get furious or very upset when the dynamic changes as they lose their grip of control.

It can feel very upsetting and painful as we let go of old relationships that no longer serve us, but it is an absolute necessity on our ever-expanding path of awakening to our soul sovereignty. Do not let sentimentality be your guide here. Clearing out old relationships that no longer serve you will allow for you to make space for new more aligned relationships to enter your life.

Eventually we only want to surround ourselves with allies who are able to walk alongside us, and who are able to truly see us in our soul's true essence. In other words, the lens that they see through is clear enough to see you shining in your power. But their lens can only be clear if they've done the necessary inner work to heal themselves. We'll begin to attract these wonderful clear-seeing souls once we've done very deep inner work on ourselves. Our relationships do act as a mirror for where we are in our consciousness.

When I was still healing aspects of my mother wound I still yearned for a best girlfriend. I wanted to still look to my female companion for reassurance, approval and love. As I healed this wound by bringing love and compassion for myself I stopped seeking this type of relationship. I simply didn't need this type of validation any longer. Once that wound healed deeply I was also able to step more deeply into my soul's purpose and start projects I'd been dreaming of for years prior. What a wonderful free feeling it was not to need anyone else's opinion or approval and to be able to just get on with my projects! I had more energy and felt more aligned than ever before. This is why it is crucial to consciously heal our mother and father wounding (explained in depth in Chapter 36, page 169), and of course, for this to happen authentically, we'll attract the perfect masculine and feminine relationships into our lives to show us where we're still in disempowerment and where we still need healing. We need to be patient and extremely observant and be willing to look deeply within to heal these old mother/father woundings. I still have deep and meaningful relationships with women, but I don't seek or need the co-dependant relationship any longer.

Eventually we only want to surround ourselves with allies who are able to walk alongside us, and who are able to truly see us in our soul's true essence.

Most of our soul's work will be brought to us via our relationships, and this is why forgiveness work, letting go of judgements, expression, guilt and shame and consciously working through our feelings especially when we're faced with conflict is extremely important. I used to want to avoid conflict, and for many years I shut down my voice in order to avoid conflict. I did this until Kundalini gave me a kick up the spine in order to find my own backbone by confronting those around me. Confrontation can bring up many fears, including the fear of judgement, rejection, abandonment, not feeling good enough, fear of upsetting others, and various other fears too. But if we choose not to confront others ever we will always be disempowered wondering what could have been, building up inner resentments, judgements, bitterness and feeling small. We must be brave and courageously confront those around us with our truth. Of course, in some situations we genuinely are called to simply walk away, especially if the other person is being aggressive or violent.

It is important to attune and discern each individual situation or relationship challenge from various different angles in order to make the best decisions. And we may make mistakes along the way, possibly by making assumptions or losing our cool due to a build-up of anger and frustration. But the point is we choose to live our lives fully by expressing our truth and our feelings in a clear way. When the emotional charge is particularly high EFT can be very helpful to calm us down *before* we confront the other person. I've done this many times, and tapped on my anger before confronting someone I felt angry with. It can help you to feel more centred, grounded and calm while maintaining firm boundaries and sticking to your guns if you need to.

The most challenging relationship will offer us an opportunity for the biggest healing and growth.

Working consciously within and alongside all of our relationships will help us to consciously evolve along our path of awakening. The most challenging relationship will offer us an opportunity for the biggest healing and growth. It is also through our current relationships that we can heal ancestral and past life wounding. If there is a past life or ancestral wounding that needs healing the soul will always bring it to us in the here and now. It is therefore very important for us to be as consciously aware as possible within all of our relationships so that we can break through old negative limiting patterns of behaviour.

I am only to look around me now to see how much I have grown spiritually speaking. My friends are not demanding of my time. In fact, they want me to listen to my body and my truth. They are approachable and willing to communicate with me and work things through. We dance, we sing, we have fun and yet we're sober getting high on life. I was synchronistically guided to a town in the west country of the UK where there is an awesome community of alternatively minded people. Sometimes I have to pinch myself to make sure I'm not just dreaming. I do feel incredibly blessed to have such a great community of soul family around me.

EFT example statements for our relationships

"Even though ... will be furious when I confront her on ..., I unconditionally love and accept myself stepping deeply into my power expressing my truth regardless."

"Even though ... is being cold and making me feel unloved, I unconditionally love and accept myself exactly as I am, knowing that I am safe and loveable."

"Even though ... judges me / wrongfully accuses me of ..., I unconditionally love and accept myself standing firmly in my power and boundaries."

"Even though ... hates me, I unconditionally love and accept myself exactly as I am."

A Prayer for our Relationships

"Mother Father Divine within, Unconditional Love, I Am Presence,

thank you for strengthening my discernment and inner trust and faith as relationships move in and out of my life with ease and grace. Thank you that I can live my life without taking any of it personally, trusting that relationships will be drawn into my life to reflect me where I am in consciousness, bringing me opportunities for growth and learning. I am grateful that all toxic and negative relationships are now drawn out of my life, while all of the unconditionally loving and supportive relationships are drawn closer to me.

It is done, and so it is. Aho/Amen/Thank You."

25

HEALING THE HEART

As we begin to heal and open our hearts more fully we not only feel more love and connection to others and life, but we also feel more of the sadness and grief that we've locked away in order to protect ourselves from feeling pain. But feeling our grief and sadness is an expression of our love and compassion. We can't have one without the other, and once our hearts are totally open we'll be open to feeling everything. In other words, it is not just 'love and light', but grief and sadness too.

Many people also misunderstand what love actually is. They seem to think that love is always open and accepting even in the face of darkness, bullying, or abuse. This is another example of false light programming that is prevalent here on Earth. Love, especially unconditional love, can be incredibly fierce and strong. If a small child is attacked by a stranger, his or her mother will fight to protect her child. Protecting ourselves and others from unconsciousness and darkness is love. Firm strong boundaries are a sign of self-love and also unconditional love. We will not allow unconsciousness or darkness to manipulate or control us or those we love as we stand up for what is right, our truth and unconditional love. Also, you can still unconditionally love the bullies and abusers and say no to their unconscious actions. This way, you are giving them an opportunity to look within and heal if they choose to. Giving your power away to the bullies is an act of low self-worth or fear. Connecting in with your heart is to connect in with your spiritual empowerment by never ever giving away your power to anyone else.

When we shut down our hearts we may cause physical disease to take hold within the physical heart and lungs. Often, it will only show up years and years later once the build-up of emotional pain has become unbearable for the physical heart. Naturally, diet has a huge impact on the physical health of the heart too, but according to my muscle testing of my clients it is more often the emotions around the heart that are the priority concerning healing.

To open the heart, we must be willing to feel our feelings. I know it can feel overwhelming and intense when we're in the process of grief, but it really is the only way that we can properly and authentically let go of the past. We must be willing to grieve our losses fully in order to move forward and grow. The more we allow ourselves to grieve and feel our sadness, the deeper we'll be able to love. Love and grief are really two sides of the same coin.

We must be willing to grieve our losses fully in order to move forward and grow. The more we allow ourselves to grieve and feel our sadness, the deeper we'll be able to love.

I remember shutting my heart down as a teenager to cope with the level of hatred and rage directed towards me on a daily basis. I had to pretend to be hard as nails to get through those years, and yet, behind closed doors I was often in floods of tears, depressed and very confused. So, I'd flip between two extreme states of being, one where I shut myself down to survive, and another where I had to catch up with the pain of what was actually going on within and around me. It was messy, and I was often labelled depressed, manic or difficult. The thing is, I did my best at the time with what I knew and with what I was facing. It is only now, more than 20 years on, that I really understand why I behaved in such dramatic and opposite ways.

Lift your voice and sing. Don't worry about getting it right or wrong. Singing has an automatic heart opening effect on the body/mind/soul. Making a continuous Aaa sound also has a healing effect on the heart.

When you are faced with the option of either listening to your mind or following your heart, I would say to always follow your heart where possible. The heart has an intelligence beyond the logic of the mind.

EFT example statements for healing the heart

"Even though ... left me, and I feel heartbroken and sad, I unconditionally love and accept myself as I am."

"I now allow myself to feel my pain and sadness, trusting that I am completely safe."

"Even though I was told or made to believe that tears are a weakness, I now unconditionally love and accept myself and my tears, knowing that it truly is a sign of my inner strength and power."

"I now easily let go of this belief that tears are a weakness from all aspects of my being."

"I now commit to opening my heart by expressing my grief and sadness."

"Even though I feel afraid to feel my feelings in case I am ridiculed, or may feel overwhelmed, I unconditionally love and accept myself and step into my power and strength by committing to the expression of my feelings."

Here you can imagine your heart opening wide to love all of you, next you can bring your heart's light (heart colours may be pink, green, golden or white) to your friends, your family, and also relationships where you've been in conflict or struggle. Finally, expand this heart light outwards, filling our planet, the Universe and All that Is. Feel your connection to everything around you, as you stay fully grounded in your body. Your prayer is now fully completed.

When you are faced with the option of either listening to your mind or following your heart, I would say to always follow your heart where possible. The heart has an intelligence beyond the logic of the mind.

A Prayer for the Heart

"Mother Father Divine within, Unconditional Love, I Am Presence,

thank you for assisting me in opening my heart. Thank you for the feelings that I am able to feel so that I can truly be alive expressing my soul's true essence including my boundaries. I am grateful for the opportunity to heal my heart this lifetime, and I commit to opening it at my own pace as I honour my feelings during my process of awakening. I now feel my heart expanding in unconditional love and I honour my feelings of grief and sadness as I step more deeply into compassion.

It is done, and so it is. Aho/Amen/Thank You."

26

HEALING THE SHADOW

There is a lot of talk about healing the shadow, but what is the shadow? We all have light and shadow within us. The shadow is what we dislike about ourselves and is usually projected outwards onto those around us as JUDGEMENTS. The shadow is also SHAME. It is basically everything we repress, deny and reject about ourselves, including our unexpressed talents and power. So how do we begin the process of healing our shame and judgements? I love using Emotional Freedom Technique to clear out shame and also to work through judgements.

We must be willing to look within and to face our shadow, not to wallow or to over process. Some people are forever 'processing' through their pain, and this can keep them trapped in victim consciousness. We must bring the light of love and acceptance to integrate and heal the shadow thoroughly, our main focus always on the solution, which is to bring love, compassion, gratitude, acceptance and healing so that we can let go and move forward with more of our true soul's essence embodied.

Some people are forever 'processing' through their pain, and this can keep them trapped in victim consciousness.

Another aspect of the shadow within is that it holds our unexpressed hidden talents and our unfulfilled potential, as we hide our soul light under a bushel. Of course, if we're in shame, fear and judgement we'll block our spiritual potential and our ability to SHINE our magnificence. I want to be shameless like the SUN and shine my light even if some may judge or reject it. I don't want to give my power away to others and cover my awesomeness any longer, and nor should you. So, when we do shadow work, not only are we called to integrate our inner shame and judgements, but we are also called to step into our talents and power, by cultivating, exploring and sharing our unique soul's gifts with the world. To heal this aspect of our shadow we'll need to put time and energy into our gifts, sharing what we love consciously with those around us. Are you expressing your inner talents and soul gifts? First you need to recognise them, then refine and cultivate these to eventually bring your unique gifts and talents to the forefront. Living our lives, expressing our gifts in this way, will inspire others to do the same. The joy we feel when we're flowing in our soul's purpose, expressing our true soul gifts, are beyond that which words can express.

As we integrate more and more of our shadow we will automatically begin to feel more self-love and acceptance, and we may begin to yearn and ache within our hearts to express more of our true selves. Eventually this desire to be our true selves will become stronger than the desire to hide. If we keep doing the daily work, going inward, working with our daily emotional triggers, and using tools such as tapping, dream-time work and meditation on a daily basis we will quickly begin to feel progress and experience lasting results. You have nothing to lose, so you may as well give it a go.

Shame

Shame has a very low energetic vibration as it is a very deep rejection of the self, and therefore becomes trapped energy within the body/mind I refer to as a major aspect of the shadow. Whatever we resist will persist, and shame is an inner resistance to parts of ourselves. It is therefore absolutely imperative to bring the light of love and acceptance to our shame wounding in order to transform it and free ourselves from the heavy deadweight grip of shame. As we begin to heal our shame, our energetic vibration will begin to rise very quickly leaving us feeling light, centred and clear in our energetic frequency.

It is due to shame and guilt that we want to hide. And when we begin to hide our desires, and who we are, it will become unconscious as we push it into darkness. Imagine if there was a platform where people could express how they really felt, even if it included wanting to harm or murder others. Just to be able to express and being heard could be incredibly healing and perhaps even prevent violence, sexual abuse and murders.

EFT example statements for shame

To clear shame you can use EFT or tapping, by tapping directly on the shame and bringing in unconditional love and acceptance for yourself. You can even tap on shame regarding any of your body parts, clearing shame around your physical appearance. You need to tap on how you see or feel it within yourself. In other words, you may not actually be overweight, but if in your mind you feel it you can tap the following,

> *"Even though I am overweight, I unconditionally love and accept myself just as I am."*

In fact, with EFT you can feel free to exaggerate your shame, anger, fear, guilt and resentments, and then watch it dissipate as you bring the light of love and acceptance to it.

Tapping this type of statement won't make you thin, but it will begin to chip away at your inner judgements and shame bringing in self-love, which in turn will help you to have stronger will-power and better self-care which may result in daily action to release excess body weight.

Another example for tapping on shame

I found myself shouting at my children when I felt very tired and they acted up emotionally, and I felt such deep shame for doing this. It also happened to be one of the things I would judge the most in other parents. How could I still be shouting at my kids when I'm a healer and helping clients heal from the effects of being shouted at as children? I felt such a deep shame and judgement around this and knew I had to tap on it. I tapped:

"Even though I shout at my children/am abusive/controlling/dominating/ fearful, I unconditionally love and accept myself as I am, and commit to changing this negative ancestral pattern within my being."

I knew exactly where this pattern came from in my ancestry. I was also guided to work with the Australian Bush remedy *Isopogon* to help with this particular issue. I also spoke to my children about this pattern, apologised and began the process of working on it by staying conscious, present and connected to them. I knew this pattern would only rear its ugly head when I felt very tired, run down and they were out of sorts too, demanding of my attention, usually at bedtime. So, I decided to look forward to feeling tired, bedtime and a few tantrums so that I could practice staying consciously patient. Another part of this particular healing was that I needed to stay consistent in my boundaries, but that I had to implement these in a calm, consistent and clear way.

A Prayer for Shame

"Mother Father Divine within, Unconditional Love, I Am Presence,

thank you for bringing your love and acceptance to all the places where I still feel shame. I understand that others who were also confused by their own shaming projected their feeling of shame on to me, and I now easily let go and forgive those who caused me to feel shame in the first place. I accept myself exactly as I am right now, as I trust in the perfection of this moment. Thank you for assisting me on my journey of awakening by bringing love and compassion to my inner rejected parts. I am deeply grateful for your assistance and guidance as I step deeper into my empowerment and myself.

It is done, and so it is. Aho/Amen/Thank You."

Judgements

I love clearing my judgements with EFT, by investigating my judgements of others and then turning it in on myself. In other words, if I felt someone else, like my partner, was really selfish I would tap:

> *"Even though I am really selfish* [and I'd even list some examples of where I'd been selfish in the past], *I unconditionally love and accept myself just as I am."*

I systematically tapped on all of my judgements of others turned in on myself, until the judgements became less and less frequent.

When I was little I was judged by my mother for being an evil child. It took me over 37 years to realise that I had to embrace and love my darkness to heal this judgement/shame. I tapped, *"Even though I am evil and dark, I unconditionally love and accept myself just as I am"*. I wept as I tapped this, and the healing was deeply profound with a huge positive impact on my life. Somewhere in my psyche I took on this belief and judgement that I was evil and shamed myself for it. I absolutely had to embrace this rejected "evil" part of myself in order to transform and heal this ancestral wound. EFT powerfully enables us to bring the light of our love and compassion to the unconscious rejected and wounded parts of ourselves. Even though I was never actually evil, a part of me did believe that I was, and punished myself for it by rejecting myself, but with the help of tapping I was able to bring the light of love and acceptance to it to deeply heal it.

> *EFT powerfully enables us to bring the light of our love and compassion to the unconscious rejected and wounded parts of ourselves.*

You'll need to be observant and very present to bring the light of consciousness to your judgements. For this reason, meditation may also greatly assist you in clearing out judgements. Forgiveness work (which I elaborate on a little later on page 162) with EFT can also be successfully applied to clear out judgements of others and ourselves.

Become observant when you're interacting with others. Watch your mind chatter and investigate your thoughts to find your judgements, and then use tapping to clear it out.

Also, be aware that pointing out a truth or using your insight, intuition and discernment is crucial along our path of awakening. People may accuse you of being judgemental when you point out a truth for instance. A friend's ex was a marijuana addict. This was a fact. But when she pointed it out to him, he would accuse her of being judgemental and demanded that she accept him exactly as he was. She believed him, and even though his marijuana addiction caused her deep stress and unrest, and also caused a division between them as he was always in a smoky haze, she bypassed her truth for many years in order to keep the peace and to stay in that relationship. What she didn't realise at the time was that she was allowing his denial of his addiction, giving away her power for fear of losing him. When she finally began to honour her own needs and her truth she was able to give him an ultimatum. He chose his addiction to marijuana and they separated. This was one of the hardest things she ever did as she genuinely loved him deeply, but she knew in the end that she was doing the right thing for her own sovereignty and spiritual empowerment.

And so sometimes you just have to call a spade a spade. In other words, you see something objectively, not because it is a projection from your own shadow wounding, and then act accordingly. There is a difference, and you'll be able to differentiate between the two as you bring more of your consciousness to your inner judgements and shame. For instance, I've worked through my own judgements and shame regarding being abusive, but this is not going to stop me from calling it out in others. Because of the love I feel for myself and humanity I have no choice but to step in to protect others and to bring the light of truth, boundaries and love to the situation. Perhaps if I was also acting from my own inner wounding I'd want to shame the perpetrators or, perhaps I'd feel drained with emotional conflict when confronting the situation, but because I've healed this wound in myself I am now able to help with fierce compassion!

Healing our shadow in our dream time

When we sleep, our unconscious minds, via dreams and nightmares, are able to process through our inner repressed and hidden aspects, or what we also refer to as the shadow. Keeping a dream journal may be very helpful to work with your unconscious mind and to come to terms with your shadow self. Eventually we can begin to train the mind to become conscious during our dreamtime so that we can investigate our shadow selves even further. It may be simpler than you think. Before you go to sleep at night state out loud that you want to become conscious during your dreams so that you can heal yourself even further at night. I have often given myself deep healings during my dreamtime. When we can become conscious within our dreams, we can also become more conscious in our day-to-day lives. Dreams can give us valuable information usually in signs and symbols to help us dislodge old stuck patterns of behaviours, fears and inner shame.

When confronted with a fearful situation or representation in our dreams or nightmares, instead of resisting it, we can integrate or heal that fearful aspect within our shadow by surrendering towards it with love and faith. You can literally hug and accept it away with love. Laugh at your demons! Focus your energy on solutions and keep the candle of faith burning strong within your heart and you will be able to spread your wings as you awaken to your soul's essence.

I also use EFT/tapping when I wake from a dream that has shown me an aspect of my shadow that needs to be healed.

Laugh at your demons! Focus your energy on solutions and keep the candle of faith burning strong within your heart ...

Astral attachments

I have personally seen and experienced how we are influenced and also affected by astral beings during our sleep or dreamtime. In order to spiritually protect ourselves from negative astral beings we need to be strong, spiritually empowered and have firm boundaries. When we are weak and in victim consciousness we may be open to the negative effects of unconscious thought forms, implants, or other astral attachments during our sleep time. But please don't panic if you find yourself being tampered with at night. It simply means you need to work on your boundaries and empowerment. All things can heal with the light of fierce love, acceptance, faith, trust and compassion.

I went through a challenging time with what I call energetic parasitic implants. I was able to feel these in my physical body. During this time, I experienced very dark nightmares and negative thoughts being dropped into my mind. I had a lot of static energy around my head, ringing in my ears and a tightness in the muscles around my jaw, ears and throat, going into my gut and into the rest of my body. These implants literally weakened my physical body. But this time period of around 4.5 years was a spiritual initiation for my soul to step more deeply into my power. A pearl is formed when a parasite or a grain of sand gets trapped within the oyster. When we're dealing with energetic parasites they always give us an opportunity to polish and develop our soul's power as we awaken to the purity of our authentic selves.

27

HEALING PAST TRAUMAS

We all have trauma. Any memory you have of an incident that makes you feel ashamed, sad, bad, fearful, angry, etc is a traumatic memory. Usually at the time of the trauma the body goes into a freeze response and the feelings we feel during the trauma go inwards and get stuck in the physical body. With more severe traumas such as accidents or violence and sexual trauma where we were victimised and felt totally disempowered the body/mind will hold the trauma, and sometimes even wipe or change the memory to cope with the level of trauma that happened. I'm going to share with you the way I cleared through all of my past traumas, including all of my sexual abuse trauma memories. I systematically worked through each memory individually, so it took me quite some time to get through them all. After clearing the trauma from these conscious memories, I used rebirthing Breathwork techniques with an experienced Breathwork practitioner to clear out the deeper more unconscious traumas and trapped emotions and was even able to heal the trauma from my own birth.

Trauma clearing method

You can do this for yourself! You need to be in a quiet and safe space though. Trust in the process and expect tears or feelings to push up to the surface as you heal and let go. Your body may shake. You may get hot or cold. It is all perfectly normal and safe. If you get panicked stop what you are doing and tap on the feeling of panic and fear until it subsides, and with tapping it will eventually completely dissipate. When fear is extreme you can tap and pace the room at the same time until you begin to feel calm, then lie down and continue tapping on the fear until it completely goes away. Always tap in safety, faith and trust when fear arises. Don't worry, you're not running away from the fear or trying to push it away. You are accepting and loving it, fully integrating it so that it can fall away naturally, as you embrace and accept it fully.

1. Think of the memory
Allow yourself to relax and think of the traumatic memory.

2. Lock it in
While thinking of the memory, use the *lock in technique* (See page 45).

3. Clear the stress
Next, I would use the *ESR Stress Release technique* (page 45) to clear the stress from that memory. Again, this is an incredibly powerful tool to remove stress from the body/mind. You need to think about the trauma memory while gently holding your ESR points.

After your biggest yawn, and still keeping the 'lock in', you can move on to Emotional Freedom Technique/Tapping.

4. EFT example statements for clearing trauma
Tap the points while making a statement like,

> *"Even though ... happened and I felt totally shocked/ angry/ashamed/fearful, I unconditionally love and accept myself and trust that I am safe."*

With sexual abuse, violence or rape memories you can add,

> *"and I claim back that part of my soul that left due to the shock and trauma"*

or

> *"and I claim back my power, or any power I gave to that individual I now claim back."*

5. Flower Essence

At this stage, you can take Bach's Rescue Remedy or Emergency Essence from the Australian Bush Remedies to assist in clearing the trauma from the body/mind.

If you experience tears, sobs or shaking, keep tapping the points until you have that release on each point. Don't stop your tapping routine or else you won't clear it properly. With some more minor traumas you may not cry, but you should experience a body signal like yawning, burping, tummy gurgles or sighing as the trauma clears. There is no set, right or wrong way of doing this. You need to just trust in the process of the clearing and witness it leave your consciousness. I used the above techniques on ALL of my conscious past traumas and felt incredibly light and clear after I cleared them all. You will FEEL the difference if you do this work thoroughly. I have also assisted hundreds of clients with these exact techniques to clear out old traumas with miraculous results.

Figure 9 recaps the Trauma Clearing method shared earlier:

Figure 9: Steps for Trauma Clearing – a recap

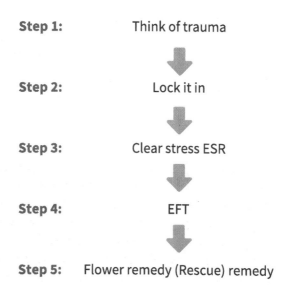

Step 1:	Think of trauma
Step 2:	Lock it in
Step 3:	Clear stress ESR
Step 4:	EFT
Step 5:	Flower remedy (Rescue) remedy

Breathwork for clearing out conscious and unconscious trauma

You can also heal past trauma with the *breath*. Breathwork can clear out conscious and unconscious traumas. The breath knows where to go, and you don't need to know why or who or what, when it comes to Breathwork. All you do is surrender into the experience so that you can allow for the breath to cleanse your emotional and physical bodies. Never underestimate the power of the breath. I've had clients say to me that their breath sessions felt more powerful than strong psychedelic plant medicines. Breathwork, when facilitated properly, can have miraculous healing effects. As the body goes into a freeze response during a trauma, in order for it to heal, the feeling that was frozen into the body has to be felt. This is why ESR, EFT and Breathwork are incredibly powerful tools to use when clearing trauma.

Never underestimate the power of the breath.

A note about psychoactive plant medicines

I would never recommend for anyone to use psychoactive plant medicines, unless they were guided to an awakened teacher/shaman via divine synchronicity. These days many people are calling themselves shamans and making huge financial profits from holding large plant medicine retreats. Many spiritual seekers are yearning for spiritual community, deeper soul connection, healing and tribe, and for these reasons feel drawn to this particular way of healing. I've seen people who only focus on this particular plant medicine work, ignoring their personal development in all other areas, and developing massive spiritual blind spots. It can be very dangerous spiritually speaking to be opened up by this strong psychoactive plant when you aren't ready for it, especially when the space you're in is not properly held in safety and care. Strong psychoactive plant medicines may also activate a premature Kundalini awakening, as it may unground the individual and may leave them open to astral possession or implantation. It is very rare to find a truly awakened shaman. I've only met one so far!

133

Also, when we expect a plant, or a guru or an ascended master or any other being or religion to fix or heal us we're not taking responsibility for our own healing. It is true that teachers and plants can guide us towards our own inner consciousness, but it is equally important not to rely solely on these teachers or plant medicines for our awakening. It is imperative that we step into our power and take ownership of ourselves by becoming conscious of our daily actions and thoughts, so that we can implement the changes we need to make in order to be radically free. Guard your being, your soul and body with great care, respect and love, and it will serve you well.

Guard your being, your soul and body with great care, respect and love, and it will serve you well.

28

HEALING SEXUAL TRAUMA

What people crave deeply is intimacy. To have true intimacy with someone else we must first become intimate with ourselves.

Most human beings on this planet, if not all of us, carry some form of sexual trauma. In fact, I believe we're all negatively affected by sexual distorted energies and sexual wounding on this planet. The trauma may be obvious such as sexual abuse, pornography addiction or rape, or it may be less obvious, perhaps just a sense of shaming around our sexuality. Because of ancestral religious shame and guilt around sex, our beliefs and feelings around sexuality are pushed down into the shadow, and have become severely distorted. The shadow side of sex can be clearly seen within the pornography industry, child sex trafficking, paedophilia and rape, where there is a victim and also a victimiser/controller involved. Often victims of sexual abuse, who have not healed or begun the process of healing themselves, can become victimisers or sexual abusers themselves.

To degrade the feminine is to degrade the masculine.

The pornography industry is booming, and unfortunately especially teenage boys and young men, but also of course girls and young women are often energetically hooked in to porn addiction. As there is still a lot of social shaming around our sexuality and we are not properly educated around the sacred practice of lovemaking and intimacy between two people who have a loving heart connection, people naturally want to educate themselves on how it all works. A genuine curiosity on top of raging new sexual hormones is motivation enough to search for porn on the Internet. And it is so easy, as all we need to do is click a few buttons on the phone or computer and there it is. The problem with pornography is that it objectifies men, women and sex. The heart is closed down, and we are programmed through these pornographic images that the orgasm is the goal and, women, more often than men, are often represented in a way where they're being controlled and overpowered. Even when porn actors and actresses claim they're sexually empowered it isn't spiritual empowerment but rather a negative fake power that is manipulative and controlling. Selling sex for money just isn't empowering.

The problem with pornography is that it objectifies men, women and sex. The heart is closed down, and we are programmed through these pornographic images that the orgasm is the goal and, women, more often than men, are often represented in a way where they're being controlled.

There are plenty of astral entities that will feed off distorted sexual addiction and energy. What tends to happen when we watch pornography is that we become desensitised to our natural way of lovemaking. We begin to need the harsh images and actions shown to us via porn to get excited sexually and to orgasm. To degrade the feminine is to degrade the masculine, and vice versa, and this is exactly what pornography does. Pornography is a result of our collective sexual wounding and shame programming. To heal ourselves from the addiction of pornography we need to be very strong and determined. It can take quite a lot of reprogramming to shift this addiction and to clear any entities or mind control devises that have been attached due to this addiction.

The pain, rage, guilt, shame and fear caused by sexual wounding becomes a food source for lower vibration entities that then latch on to its host spiking him or her with dark thoughts and distorted sexual images to perpetuate the trauma so that it can keep feeding off the pain and misery caused. These entities and implants can make it very difficult to break out of the victim/victimiser programming, negative sexual thinking and behaviours. To heal these wounds, this darkness and this sexual distortion inside, we need to bring the light of our compassion, acceptance and love to it. EFT is a great tool for doing just this. Here are a few examples of what you can tap concerning sexual wounding.

EFT example statements for sexual wounding

"Even though I am perverted and have perverted thoughts, I unconditionally love and accept myself just as I am."

You may not actually be a pervert, but when we exaggerate during tapping it can amplify the healing process. Bringing love and acceptance to our own perversions will allow for these to naturally fall away. Also, thinking of our own perversions will usually bring up shame, showing us that we need to heal this part of our shadow.

"Even though my body lusts for ..., I unconditionally love and accept myself just as I am."

It can feel scary or out of control when our body is responding sexually in a way we may not want it to respond.

"Even though I am addicted to watching pornography, I unconditionally love and accept myself just as I am."

"Even though I was sexually abused, I unconditionally love and accept myself, and I now trust that I am safe."

"Even though I was sexually abused, I now claim back my soul, and I trust that it is safe for me to say NO."

"Even though I will upset the other person when I say no, I now commit to

strengthening my boundaries and saying no regardless of how they feel."

"I now honour my sexuality as a woman/man and only allow healthy and loving relationships into my life who honour me."

When it comes to EFT regarding sexual abuse and trauma, we will have to tap on all of our traumatic memories around the abuse, and bring in self-love and acceptance, faith in the process, safety and also eventually we'll need to tap ourselves out of victim consciousness into full forgiveness and personal power to finally heal it completely.

It often takes many years to heal our sexual wounding, but with time and patience we can do it. You can also heal sexual wounding if you're in a conscious relationship during your own love making, but you'll both need to be very present and compassionate and allow for yourselves to be completely vulnerable as you bring love and acceptance in for each other and yourselves.

STD's, infertility, impotence, hormonal disorders

STD's, emotionally speaking, relate to our collective shame and guilt around our sexuality and there is no doubt in my mind that religion, with its shame and fear mongering, is the major cause of sexual shame and trauma on this planet.

Infertility, Impotence and other related hormonal disorders often relate to heavy metal, parasitic, Candida and astral parasitic toxicity, and also emotional or mental blockages or past sexual trauma. Much of our sexual trauma is passed down through the ancestry. So often people who were raped or sexual abused have children who also then experience rape or abuse. There is an abused victimised and disempowered energetic frequency that the perpetrators can feel or sense. This is again why stepping into our spiritual BOUNDARIES is absolutely key in healing our sexuality. We simply must claim back our power if we want to heal this negative sexual imprint!

Sexual purification

We do need to purify our sexuality if we are serious about full soul purification. This may mean that you go without sex for a few years. It of course depends on your own personal journey regarding sexual trauma and whether you are awakening with a partner or on your own. But there is a reason why many spiritual masters abstained from sex according to ancient spiritual texts. Sex can be massively addictive, and a distraction along our path of soul embodiment. If we cannot master ourselves sexually we will remain confused and scattered energetically speaking. Of course, we must not repress our sexuality either! But sexuality can be explored in various different ways, not only by having sex with others.

Stepping into our spiritual BOUNDARIES is absolutely key in healing our sexuality.

We need to embrace, accept and love our sexuality but at the same time not allow for it to take us over. You cannot be a slave to your sexual urges and expect to awaken and marry your divine masculine and feminine within. Respect yourself, your body, and your sexuality and express your creativity and sexuality through art, music, dance, etc. When you masturbate do it as an act of respectful self-love, and practice doing it with a clear mind focusing on your breath and your body. Gift yourself with orgasm as a sign of self-care and self-love rather than mindless addictive behaviour that happens daily due to habit. At the same time, if you are addicted to porn or/and masturbation, don't judge yourself, just start to accept yourself fully, while you begin the process of healing your sexual wounding bit by bit. Eventually, just like a smoker giving up cigarettes, your urge to stop watching pornography will become greater than your urge to watch or partake in it.

I've witnessed how in certain spiritual New Age circles there are couples that swap partners or have what is referred to as open relationships or free love. This may feel very grown up or spiritually advanced, but I can tell you now from my own experience and from what I have witnessed over the years that this type of relationship usually gets very messy. When we have sex with someone we exchange parts of ourselves. Sex is a sacred act and creates an energetic tie or bond with our sexual partner. Entities and implants can get transferred between people during sex. DNA gets passed from one person to the other. Many people are deeply wounded and having sex with other deeply wounded people, often with closed hearts, continues the cycle of pain. If you are unable to be intimate with yourself or be silent and at peace with stillness within yourself, then you will not be able to be intimate with anyone else in a deep and connected way. When you disconnected from yourself you may get bored easily, wanting to experiment with multiple partners or open relationships. This may continue for you until you begin to do the inner healing work required for your soul to unify and become radically free. But if we're still a slave to our sexual impulses, then until we begin this process of soul purification, we will remain stuck in cycles of sexual confusion and pain.

We need to embrace, accept and love our sexuality but at the same time not allow for it to take us over. You can't be a slave to your sexual urges and expect to awaken and marry your divine masculine and feminine within. Respect yourself, your body, and your sexuality and express your creativity and sexuality through art, music, dance, etc.

When we truly love and honour ourselves we will have strong boundaries and we'll be unafraid to express these before, during and after sex. Sexual boundaries are a sign of self-love and care.

Sex, when used consciously with an open heart and a loving partner, is incredibly healing and a powerful connecter between two souls. It is a powerful, magical, enlightening source of energy, and when used with mindfulness and presence can be a catalyst for spiritual healing and awakening. But we need to go back to the basics, into the purity of our hearts, our inner yearning to be truly met with love and acceptance on all levels of our being. Give yourself to one person until that connection ends naturally. I would then advise to purify yourself of resentments, guilt, pain, shame, obligations or any other energy that tied you to your previous partner, before getting sexually involved with another person. Be totally at peace when you're making love and when you're not making love, whether you're with a partner or single. And when you are single, enjoy your sexual energy and express it through dance, music, movement of any sorts, wearing sexy clothing, or express your creativity doing what you love.

Sex is a divine expression of creative energy, and also bringing us a much-deserved opportunity to give and receive pleasure while being intimate with our partner and ourselves.

Sex is our ultimate creative force and deserves to be respected and celebrated. It is a divine expression of creative energy, and also bringing us a much-deserved opportunity to give and receive pleasure while being intimate with our partner and ourselves. As we become conscious and more present sexually, we will be able to experience a lot more long-lasting pleasure. Oh, if only people really knew!! They'd chuck out their porn stash and sign up to Vipassana silent and meditation retreats instead!

29

HEALING THE INNER CHILD

The *inner child* is the little boy or girl who was unable to respond to traumatic events or incidents and who then stayed trapped inside as the broken child within. Feeling unheard and unloved by YOU, your inner child will begin to rebel by throwing their emotional toys out of the pram even when you're now in a grown-up body. To heal our inner child we need to be willing to revisit our childhood traumatic memories and to give our child what it is he or she needs to feel empowered, heard and healed. *Matrix Reimprinting*, which is a technique that was born out of EFT can work miraculous wonders with inner child healing. As we tap the meridian points we take ourselves into the memory where the trauma occurred and we ask our child what it is he or she needs. This type of work is usually best with an experienced practitioner, as it can feel incredibly emotional.

With Inner Child healing we are integrating lost parts of ourselves back into ourselves with love and compassion.

Once the child feels heard and loved, and able to also express themselves, and once the trauma is cleared thoroughly with ESR and EFT then the healing will be completed. All the inner child wants is to be seen, heard and held compassionately. It needs to be able to express perhaps what it couldn't at the time of the trauma. You'll need to be patient with your inner child as it begins to build trust in you and the Divine. With Inner Child healing we are integrating lost parts of ourselves back into ourselves with love and compassion.

My inner child used to throw massive emotional tantrums when I felt unloved by my previous partners. My little girl inside, who felt so unworthy of being loved due to the emotional neglect I felt from my parents, raged and cried as an adult whenever this past pain was triggered. All my little girl wanted and needed was reassurance and of course I only attracted partners who would walk out on me when I was in distress. My soul kept recreating the trauma bringing me the opportunity to heal and transcend the negative pattern. I was stuck in this painful cycle for many years, and it only really healed once I was able to give myself the love and reassurance I so deserved. I healed this cycle of pain using EFT daily for quite a few years bringing in love and acceptance to my little girl who felt so deeply unloved and unworthy of love.

EFT example statements for Inner Child Healing

"Even though I was unheard, or felt unloved, unseen, etc by … when I was a child [or think of specific memory for best results], *I unconditionally love and accept myself exactly as I am, and I trust in the process of life and that I am safe."*

A Prayer for the Inner Child

"Mother Father God/Goddess, All that Is,

thank you for healing my inner child who felt afraid/unloved/ unworthy, [or *whatever emotion it brings up*], when [*name specific memory or incident*] happened. I now flood my broken child with the light of unconditional love and compassion and I give him/her back his/her power. Thank you that this is done now.

It is done, and so it is. Aho/Amen/Thank You

30

BOUNDARIES AND SELF-WORTH

Having 100% strong energetic boundaries is an act of unconditional fierce empowered love. Remember, love is not just 'focusing on the positive', it is also a fierce 'NO' to unconscious or negative energy, as we only allow loving and kind energy to surround us and those we love. But saying no, and expressing our truth and our boundaries requires us to love ourselves and to feel worthy. Therefore, working on our boundaries, we are automatically working on our self-esteem. Do you love yourself enough to say 'No'? Do you love yourself enough to express your truth beyond any shadow shaming that may arise for feeling your lower emotional responses such as fear, anger or guilt? Do we love ourselves enough to express righteous anger in the moment when needed?

Do you love yourself enough to say 'No'?

I had to do a lot of tapping on expression and boundaries as I was completely shut down due to strong social and ancestral conditioning. The main beliefs I had to break through was, "*I must not upset others*", "*I need to keep the peace and keep safe*", "*I'll be judged or rejected if I really express my truth*", "*I'll be a bad person if my truth upsets the other person*", "*Their needs are more important than my own, and this makes me a good spiritual person*". It took me a few years to fully break through this conditioning and to find the courage to begin to express my truth. Sometimes my truth came out all wrong and it did upset the other person. Other times I was totally surprised when I expressed and was drawn closer to the other person for allowing myself to be seen in my vulnerabilities and truth. With each opportunity for honest heart-felt expression I grew in strength and courage. I began to research communication skills such as Non-Violent Communication. This helped me to communicate in a clear and constructive way, and to also be able to really listen to others.

When we don't have any boundaries, we'll attract parasitic personalities towards us. We will also attract parasites in our physical bodies and parasitic attachments in the astral or 4th dimensional realm. It is therefore incredibly important to work on our boundaries. Having a boundary doesn't mean you're in fear. It simply means you know what is good for you and what isn't, and that you respond to your inner feelings and your inner truth with fierce compassion and love. If we shut our truth and ability to communicate down how can we ever trust ourselves? **We can only trust ourselves if we respond to our inner feelings and express them in the moment.** And when we can't trust ourselves we're lost and disempowered.

Part of the false light programming on this planet will have us all believe that boundaries are fear-based and bad, and that we should be completely open and accepting of everyone and everything. This is a blatant false light lie that will keep humans open to negative astral influence and attack. When we have no boundaries and we allow for people to harm others or ourselves we actually coerce with that distorted negative energy, allowing for the darkness to reign. True unconditional love will fiercely stand up for the truth, while expressing our limitations, and also feel compelled to do so for others.

EFT example statements for boundaries

"Even though ... shouted at me and I did nothing, I unconditionally love and accept myself and I now step deeply into my boundaries, knowing that it is safe for me to express my 'No'."

"Even though ... may reject me or cause a fight when I express my truth, I unconditionally love and accept myself and commit to expressing my truth regardless of how it makes others feel."

"I now allow myself to express my boundaries as I step deeply into my power as a man/woman."

"Even though my partner or ... lives at a much faster pace than me, it is now easy for me to stay grounded, centred and present within my own soul's rhythm and boundaries."

A Prayer for Boundaries

"Mother Father Divine within, Unconditional Love, I Am Presence,

thank you for assisting me in strengthening my boundaries. I now step deeply into my courage as I practice saying no and set and express my limits with those around me. I remove all parasitic, controlling and manipulative relationships from my life with fierce compassion and assertiveness. Thank you for assisting me as I step deeper into the truth of whom I am, how I feel and expressing my desires and what I don't want. I am strong, powerful, have clear and firm boundaries and am free.

It is done, and so it is. Aho/Amen/Thank You."

31

SELF-LOVE

Self-love is *self-care*. It is resting when we're tired, or investing time towards the things we genuinely love to do. It is mindfulness, and consciously changing our negative self-talk by being more loving and intimate with ourselves. Self-love is also a form of coming home to ourselves, enjoying silence, stillness and our own company. Spending time alone can be deeply healing and precious. Lift your voice if you like to sing, go for a walk if you love to be in nature and paint if you love art. Do what makes you feel joy and love. Start to get into the habit of prioritising your own needs, and looking after yourself. When you really begin to self-care your boundaries will naturally strengthen. If you don't love YOU how can you love anyone else? The deeper I am able to love myself, the deeper I can love you. It really does start within.

Self-love is also a form of coming home to ourselves, enjoying silence, stillness and our own company.

If your self-esteem is low, you'll be disempowered and most probably also in victim consciousness. Low self-esteem or self-worth is what the ego feeds off, separating itself, comparing, putting itself below or above others all due to low self-worth. Most people do not want others to know that they suffer this wound and will cover it up with masks of perfectionism, intellectualism, or materialism. Low self-esteem also causes addictions, self-harming and other destructive behaviours and mental disorders.

EFT example statement for self-love

> *"Even though he/she hates me, I unconditionally love and accept myself as I am."*

> *"Even though she said I was worthless* [think of specific memory], *I unconditionally love and accept myself as I am."*

But how do we love ourselves when we've never been shown love, or if we don't even know what it feels like to be loved? I've been working on my self-esteem consciously with EFT for nearly 15 years, and even though it is still a process, it really does work miraculously to bring the light of love and compassion to all of ourselves. Every single time we tap: *"I unconditionally love and accept myself"* it sinks in a little deeper. Tapping on shame will raise your self-esteem very quickly. Tap on what makes you cringe about yourself. This way you'll get the best results.

> *"Even though I have a flabby tummy/a large nose/pimples, I unconditionally love and accept myself exactly as I am."*

Loving ourselves is *an inside job*, and the more we can bring love and acceptance to ourselves, especially to our inner rejected parts, the more we'll begin to attract others who will love us unconditionally too. And the more we love ourselves, the more we will be able to love others. Learning to love all of ourselves including our shadow is teaching us to unconditionally love ourselves and those around us.

Low self-esteem also causes addictions, self-harming and other destructive behaviours and mental disorders.

A Prayer for Self-Love

"Mother Father Divine within, Unconditional Love, I Am Presence,

thank you for helping me love ALL of myself unconditionally. I now choose to take care of myself daily and to respond to my own inner needs with care and compassion. I feel your Divine unconditional love for me knowing that I deserve to be loved on all levels of my being. I now give to you any painful traumatic memories where I was shamed, so that they can be washed clean by your unconditional love and acceptance. Thank you for assisting me along this journey of self-love.

It is done, and so it is. Aho/Amen/Thank You."

32

REGRET

To heal regret, we need to strengthen our trust and faith in life, the Divine and ourselves as we also forgive life and ourselves for whatever happened in the past. When we make so-called mistakes they will always bring us opportunities for spiritual growth. There is ALWAYS a gift/learning attached to any challenging situation we face, even if you're only able to see it years later. Judging yourself to be a failure for past 'mistakes' won't do you or anyone else any good.

Regret, like guilt and shame, is a form of SELF-HARM as we are continuously beating ourselves up for things that happened in the past, wondering why we didn't act differently at the time. When we're in regret we're disempowered and in victim, unable to move forward to embrace life fully.

So how do we break through this self-harming cycle of regret? We break through by accepting and forgiving ourselves for what occurred in the past. We grieve our losses and then we will be able to authentically move forward feeling free to be ourselves, mistakes and all.

EFT can certainly speed up the process of clearing regret from the body/mind.

EFT example statements for regret

"Even though I did ... and I feel such deep regret, I unconditionally love and accept myself and my feelings as I trust in life, myself and the Divine."

"I now trust that I am exactly where I am meant to be, and am grateful for

what [the situation] *has taught me. I claim back my power."*

"Even though I feel so angry with myself for what I said/did ..., I unconditionally love and accept myself and my feelings exactly as I am."

"Even though I feel afraid that I won't learn my lesson if I let go of this inner hatred/anger/resentment/regret, I now trust that I can forgive myself and still learn the lesson at hand."

"Even though I feel so small and disempowered due to how I behaved ..., I unconditionally love and accept myself and I take full responsibility for my life, claiming back my power as I forgive myself fully for how I reacted."

A Prayer for Regret

"Mother Father Divine within, Unconditional Love, I Am Presence,

thank you for assisting me in letting go of this regret within my being. I am grateful for what this situation has taught me, and I now fully accept this learning as a gift for my soul's growth. I commit to loving, accepting and forgiving myself on all levels for any mistakes I may have made in the past. I am grateful that this regret is teaching me to make important changes. I now make the necessary changes within my life so that I can be fully free from all regret. I trust in the process of Life, the Divine and myself.

It is done, and so it is. Aho/Amen/Thank You."

33

GUILT AND OBLIGATIONS

Guilt and obligations can also be seen in the astral or 4th dimensional realm as negative ties and hooks between people. If you want to be radically free it will be essential to clear out guilt and obligations along your path. It can be very challenging to clear obligations we feel, especially towards family members. Some cultures seem to have deeper family obligations than others. In many ways, if you had a challenging childhood like mine was, it can be easier to let go of family obligations, than if your childhood was a happy one. I've seen parents manipulate their grown-up children to no end by being very 'nice' (false light), keeping their children close in order to feel more in control or better about themselves.

Manipulative energy

An example of manipulative energy is, *"You do this for me, and then I'll love you, support you and be there for you"*. This type of dynamic or energy is extremely common in families and it is a good example of conditional love. Money is often used to control and manipulate, just as the energy of withholding love and affection can be used. When we're doing things for others out of guilt or obligation we're disempowered, hooked into a negative cycle and giving our energy to them.

When we're doing things for others out of guilt or obligation we're disempowered, hooked into a negative cycle and giving our energy to them.

To be radically free we will have to begin the process of clearing guilt and obligations. We may need to do some deep clearing regarding our fears, as we ask ourselves the question what may happen if we really did what felt right and good for us. We'll need to be willing to lose family members or friendships as we step deeper into our truth and authenticity. Do you want to live your life for others and their needs, or do you want to live your soul's true divine purpose?

EFT example statements for guilt and obligations

It was incredibly hard to leave my ex-husband due to 11 years of being in partnership, marriage vows and two children. One of the most powerful EFT taps I did was the following:

> *"Even though I will lose his love for me when I leave him, I unconditionally love and accept myself just as I am."*

I sobbed while I tapped this statement and it helped me to step deeply into my inner strength and to walk away from a relationship that no longer served me. I needed to break free to be myself, and part of the process was clearing obligations and guilt.

One of the statements I tapped often regarding guilt was:

> *"Even though I feel guilty for separating our family and taking the children away with me, I unconditionally love and accept myself as I trust in the process of my healing journey and that this is for all of our highest and best."*

Even with daily tapping it still took me around a year to clear the guilt for leaving that relationship. We need to be persistent as we heal ourselves.

There are many healers who talk about cord cutting, and they will give you all sorts of meditations to do this for yourself, but from my own personal experience I can tell you now that it is all a waste of time unless you clear out the obligations, guilt, resentments and fears that still keep you attached to the other person. Tapping has helped me authentically let go and forgive everyone from my past. It is such

153

a powerful tool, especially when coupled with long hours of meditation and also Breathwork sessions.

Some more EFT statements concerning guilt and obligations

"Even though they will judge me for being selfish if I don't go to or do ... [the obligation], I unconditionally love and accept myself and step into my power and truth regardless of how others see or judge me."

"Even though I feel such guilt around not seeing my parents this Christmas, I unconditionally love and accept myself and I express my truth and my needs regardless."

"Even though I'll be hated for ..., I unconditionally love and accept myself as I step into my power and my boundaries."

And as you step deeper into your power, letting go of guilt and obligations you most probably will lose friendships or relationships. We need to be utterly willing to stand alone in order to step into our authentic spiritual empowerment and radical freedom. Eventually we will attract others who are also in their power, and who will love us for being true to ourselves.

34

CLEARING FEAR BLOCKAGES

And when you're alone there's a very good chance
You'll meet things that scare you right out of your pants
There are some, down the road between hither and yon
That can scare you so much you won't want to go on.
                    Dr Seuss,
                    'Oh the Places You'll Go'.

It is perfectly normal and even important for us to have some fear so that we wouldn't fall off cliffs or walk into on-coming traffic. I am not addressing this type of fear here. In this section I am concerned with unconscious fears that limit your soul's expression from being RADICALLY FREE.

Fear is usually a response of resistance to a past trauma that then replays itself during our day-to-day in various unconscious ways. I recently choked on some food and really struggled to get air into my lungs. I had to throw myself on all fours, gag and cough to be able to start breathing again. I really felt the feeling of choking and not being able to breathe and it caused a panic within my being. That same night, every time I drifted off to sleep I'd stop breathing for a moment and then wake with a start. The trauma of choking had caused a fear response that needed healing. I began to tap on this fear of dying, losing myself and/or losing my children, bringing in love, acceptance and faith in the process of life and death. After one round of in-depth tapping I fell into a deep and peaceful sleep. I also felt that this choking episode had to happen for me to clear through this deep fear as it all coincided with an inner death of my old self. In any case this episode brought me an opportunity to clear through the fear of being out of control, dying or losing myself.

Fear acts like a magnet and will attract the very thing it is we are afraid of.

Fear acts like a magnet and will attract the very thing it is we are afraid of. If, for instance, we have a deep fear of being rejected we may find ourselves being rejected over and over again until we learn to love and accept ourselves fully. Or sometimes people withhold information as they think it will hurt the other person, only for that person to then find out and to be hurt that they were never told in the first place! I was once really afraid to confront someone about something and I didn't say anything. All this time the energy around it built and eventually, after three months of not saying anything I found myself confronting this person via text message. To her, my confrontation came out of the blue and felt over the top, and it caused a huge row. Exactly what I felt afraid of happened, and it was caused by my fear in the first place! To be fairer to myself, I'm not sure how she would have responded three months prior to this event as she was incredibly unapproachable and easily triggered. Nevertheless, she brought me the perfect opportunity to heal this fear of expression/ confrontation, for being judged or rejected.

The only way to clear fear is to accept that we have the fear in the first place. As fear arises in the body allow it to be there. Investigate it and tap on it. EFT is more powerful than any anti-anxiety drug you can purchase from the pharmacy. It is a tool you can use instantly as panic, anxiety or fear arises.

EFT example statements for fear of being out of control
The fear of losing control often sits at the root of many other minor or superficial fears and phobias. We can tap on this fear in the following way.

"Even though I am out of control due to ..., I trust that I am exactly where I am meant to be and that I am safe."

Now you can think of memories where you felt out of control and afraid, or where you experienced trauma and tap through these with the statement,

"Even though I was out of control when the trauma happened, I now trust that I am completely safe. I trust in life, myself and the Divine."

With EFT, it is important to tap on all of our past traumas individually where fear originated and to tap in safety, faith and trust.

Whenever you are trying to control a situation or a person you are in FEAR.

Whenever you are trying to control a situation or a person you are in FEAR. Control and fear go hand in hand, so when you see someone who is displaying controlling behaviour you can know that they're acting from a place of deep and often unconscious fear. For instance, Obsessive Compulsive Disorder (OCD) or Anorexia Nervosa are two mental disorders that are based around control. This need to control the environment or one's food intake is always based on deep unconscious fear programming, and usually during healing we'd have to go to the original trauma to do a clearing and healing on this fear.

EFT example statements for fear
I'd tap something to this effect when I feel fear or panic,

"Even though I feel really afraid right now about ..., I unconditionally love and accept myself and I trust that I am safe, I trust myself, life and the Divine."

It is incredibly miraculous how quickly tapping will calm the adrenals and clear the fear. I'm still amazed at the power of this little tool for feelings that can feel so incredibly out of control, big and scary.

To clear fear from the past you can apply the following statement,

"Even though ... happened and I felt so scared/ terrified/ out of control, I unconditionally love and accept myself and my feelings, and I trust that I am safe."

Phobia

A phobia, like for instance a spider phobia, is never really about spiders, even though to the person with the phobia they will usually feel utterly terrified and even frozen in fear when confronted with one. Usually a phobia represents a deeper fear of being out of control. I'm still amazed at how quickly and easily one can clear a phobia with EFT.

EFT example statements for phobia

Think of the phobia. For instance, think of a spider if you have a spider phobia and tap,

"Even though I'm afraid of spiders, I unconditionally love and accept myself and I trust that I am safe."

Look at a photo or a picture of a spider and tap the same statement. You can also tap,

"Even though I'm so afraid of being out of control, this spider may jump on me, I trust in the process of life, myself and life. I trust that I am safe."

If you can, actually have a real spider nearby or in a container and tap while moving closer towards it. Every time you get afraid stay there and tap until the fear goes, and then move closer to it again. You can do this until you're right in front of the spider.

Embracing your fears

Whatever we resist will persist. Remember, the soul just wants to be free, so it will bring you all of your fears, fear for fear, in order for you to face it and heal it. We can either ignore our fears or pretend they're not there and never grow, or we can begin to work with them, confronting them and stepping deeper into our power and freedom. Before my Kundalini awakening I avoided my fears, running the other way, not even wanting to think about them in case I'd have to feel them. I kept sending my fears to the light, but that never worked. I am so deeply grateful for EFT, as it really became my 'go to' tool when fear raised its dark uncomfortable head. EFT ALWAYS works if we tap thoroughly and in the way I have suggested here in this book. EFT is simply reprogramming your unconscious mind by bringing love, acceptance and faith to your fears. Instead of pushing them away you're facing them, expressing them with your statement and transmuting them with your full acceptance, love and faith.

EFT ALWAYS works if we tap thoroughly and in the way I have suggested here in this book. EFT is simply reprogramming your unconscious mind by bringing love, acceptance and faith to your fears.

You can also use the tool of *meditation* to work through your fears. Go into a deep space of stillness and meditation and invite one of your fears to be with you. Feel it with your whole being fully meeting it and watch it dissolve. Don't push it away or try for it to fade or dissolve, it will happen naturally as you fully accept it in your body.

If I'm holding a breath circle and someone is experiencing fear and their body shakes, spasms or contorts, I get them in touch with their anger and rage by suggesting for them to make sound. Anger will empower you and can pull you out of the vibration of fear very quickly. Usually once they've raged for a while the tears will come as the energy shifts into grief, and so that finally the energy of fear and trauma can fully move out of the body. It is an incredibly powerful process to hold and witness in myself and for others.

Be persistent

In my experience, some deep-rooted fears will keep emerging again and again for healing as you go along your path of awakening. Every time you feel the fear, just feel it, breathe and know that it is just fear.

EFT will assist in clearing it out quicker than any other modality I've ever worked with. It works every time if you're tapping in the right way. Sometimes you need to be a little patient, especially if you're in a state of panic. Pace the floor and keep tapping, and trust that it will pass. It is only a feeling, and feelings always pass. It is when we resist feelings that they persist, and this is of course exactly what fear is, resistance. You need to get yourself
back into faith and trust, and tapping is by far the quickest and easiest way to do this.

Figure 10: Observing the Moment from Fear to Freedom

FEAR

ANGER

GRIEF

RELIEF

Food and fear

Food intolerances and *toxins* caused from Candida, parasites or heavy metals can also cause anxiety and fear. Detoxing from these toxins can bring up anxiety or an unsettled feeling within the body/mind. Know that it does pass as the toxins leave the physical body. Liver cleansing herbs like milk thistle and dandelion can be very helpful to prevent this type of anxiety while also drinking a lot of water to purify.

Empower yourself

As an antidote to fear you can watch and listen to the Indigenous war cry, *the Hakka*, to get yourself into a space of courage and strength. When we are strong physically, perhaps pushing some weights at the gym, or exercising regularly, our emotional, mental and spiritual bodies will also be strong. However, when the body is swimming in parasitic or fungal toxicity it can cause anxiety and fear as we're in a disempowered state of being. This is another great reason to keep your physical body and specifically your gut, in balance by detoxing regularly and keeping healthy, strong, clear and fit

35

FORGIVENESS

I am so incredibly excited to be sharing this forgiveness work with you. It is incredibly empowering and will free you from the past. But remember too that forgiveness takes time and is a process, and the time this process takes deserves to be honoured, not shamed. The more conscious we get around this forgiveness process the easier it will be for us to get to our final goal of forgiveness. Forgiveness is not so much about the other person as it is about personal freedom and empowerment. When we sit with resentment in our body/mind we are disempowered and in victim consciousness. You may really want to forgive but feel you're unable to do so, not even knowing where to begin the process. If you are really serious about wanting to forgive though, you can follow the following tapping sequence on each specific resentment and watch how your life changes for the better.

EFT example statements for forgiveness
I use EFT/tapping to speed up the process of forgiveness with the following four steps:

Step 1: I'd tap on the actual resentment/incident. The more specific you are the more powerfully this will work for you.

There will often be more than one aspect you feel angry or resentful over. Pick the one with the biggest emotional charge and start there. You'll have to work through each aspect individually as you go through these steps.

"Even though he did … and I feel angry/resentful, I unconditionally love and accept myself and my feelings just as I am." [Remember to be very specific here]

Now, you may also be called to confront the person here, so don't use EFT to deny this important step of confrontation if it is what is called for. You will have to discern whether confrontation would be necessary or useful here or not. EFT will make the confrontation much easier though as you can get your emotional charge down and communicate in a more grounded or diplomatic way.

On the other hand, you may be tapping here as you have already confronted the other person and perhaps they were unable to hear you and said some hurtful things to you too. Tap individually on your emotional triggers here bringing in love and acceptance for yourself. In other words, if something hurt your feelings it is usually because on some level you fear or believe it yourself. EFT will help you clear out all of your emotional triggers if you consistently tap on these daily. More on this topic on page 31 and throughout the book.

Step 2: I'd tap on the fear of the other person getting away with what they did or said if I do let go of the resentment or anger, and bring in that I trust in divine justice.

"Even though I'm afraid she will get away with it, if I let go of my resentment, I now trust in divine justice and that it is safe for me to let it go."

Step 3: I'd tap myself out of victim into gratitude for what it is the situation is teaching me. In other words, I'm tapping myself back into full empowerment.

"Even though I feel like a victim because of what she did …, I am now deeply grateful that this situation has brought me the following learnings [name these]. *I take full responsibility for my part in this argument, and I claim back any power I may have given her over me."*

Step 4: Finally, I'd make the choice to forgive. Sometimes I tap this, and other times I just have to make the choice to really feel it cementing the release.

> *"I now choose to forgive ... as I trust that it is safe for me to let go of what she did."*

It is important to use these steps on each aspect of the incident separately. It is not a simple process and takes time even with this powerful technique. If you are determined and really want to forgive you'll get there in the end, but to authentically do it in my experience it does take time and effort. Sometimes there are deeper karmic lessons at hand that we're still in process of working through and learning. Some incidents are not straightforward and there may be a going backwards and forwards to deeply heal past wounding.

This process of forgiveness can of course also be applied to ourselves, especially concerning feelings of guilt and regret.

> ### *Sometimes there are deeper karmic lessons at hand that we're still in process of working through and learning.*

This work right here on forgiveness is some of the most powerful work I've ever done on myself and for my clients. It will change your life and raise your energetic spiritual vibration faster than you can imagine. If you are working through resentment with these steps and still feel it is very difficult to forgive, don't beat yourself up. Keep tapping and don't give up. I've managed to forgive everyone in my life and myself with the above four steps. The freedom and empowerment of forgiveness is well worth working towards. Awakening is after all about YOUR freedom!

Once you've worked through all of your resentments you'll find it much easier to forgive in the moment. You won't take things so personally anymore, and you'll begin to cultivate a deep sense of compassion for others. Being free from fear, resentment and victim consciousness is a massive relief on the soul, and once we really experience the joy of forgiveness we'll want to pass it on to others.

Figure 11: Using EFT for Forgiveness Work

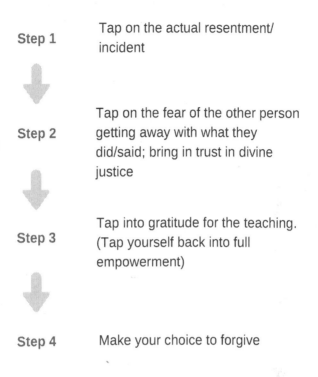

Step 1	Tap on the actual resentment/ incident
Step 2	Tap on the fear of the other person getting away with what they did/said; bring in trust in divine justice
Step 3	Tap into gratitude for the teaching. (Tap yourself back into full empowerment)
Step 4	Make your choice to forgive

Forgiveness does not mean we're allowing others to walk all over us. I have forgiven my maternal grandfather for sexually abusing me but have chosen to never see him again. The reason for this is that he never took responsibility for what he did. He never apologised. Why would I want to allow someone into my life when they've harmed me and have refused to acknowledge it? I wouldn't be doing him or myself any favours. At the same time, I genuinely feel deep compassion for him and for what he has had to carry in this lifetime. I don't even want to think about what he had to endure as a child. I forgive him, and I'm free from having to carry all the pain and trauma from the past.

Forgiveness does not mean we're allowing others to walk all over us.

One of the things that I experienced when I was able to forgive others was that often unconsciously it would affect the other person. For instance, I'd forgive someone and then the next day I'd bump into them somewhere really random and they'd be in a really open heart space too. Or it happened once that I forgave someone and that they called me within hours with most beautiful voice message on my phone of how they missed me. Forgiveness is incredibly powerful and will shift your life in miraculous ways.

Forgiveness is EMPOWERMENT 🌐

A Prayer for Forgiveness

"Mother Father Divine within, Unconditional Love, I Am Presence,

Thank you for assisting me in the process of forgiving all of those people who have hurt me in the past. I am deeply grateful for the lessons and the learning as I trust in Divine Justice and that it is sage for me to let the past go.

It is done, and so it is. Amen/Aho/Thank You."

From Victim Consciousness to being Fully Sovereign, free and empowered

This is an essential step during our forgiveness work, but so incredibly important in terms of our empowerment I feel I need to write about it a little further here.

You can apply EFT and tap yourself systematically out of victim consciousness. This is exactly what I did. Every single time you think, *"Why did this happen to me?"*, *"Poor me"*, *"Why me?"*, etc you have an opportunity to pull yourself out of victim consciousness with tapping.

It is true that we have been victimised at times in our lives, and that we were victims then. Part of our journey of freeing ourselves is to eventually take responsibility for how we grow and learn from the experience. It doesn't mean the other party should be let off the hook, as we may be called to take further action in terms of justice and honouring our truth and boundaries! It doesn't mean that you CONSCIOUSLY did it to yourself either or that you're condoning the other person's behaviour! We also don't jump to empowerment/forgiveness prematurely! Honour yourself for where you are in your PROCESS of empowerment. We cannot say to someone who is still processing through their feelings of victimisation, shock and trauma that they should forgive or take responsibility! Too often I've heard people doing this, and even though it may come from a well-meaning place, it sounds incredibly judgemental, while invalidating the person's pain and suffering. Think before you speak! Hearing someone in pain with no agenda to fix or heal them can be incredibly healing for them, and help them to authentically move themselves out of that disempowered victimised place.

When we trust in life and ourselves we can allow ourselves to be moved by life.

*It c*an be very helpful and empowering to see our lives from a higher perspective where we are co-creating with life/the Divine/All that Is. Perhaps a higher aspect of ourselves has brought us the situation via the law of cause and effect or karma so that we can thoroughly heal it, let go, grow and move forward. When we truly understand and integrate this as inner knowing we can let go of victim consciousness and begin to step deeply into our soul sovereignty, inner faith, trust and freedom.

This doesn't mean we're taking responsibility for what others have done! It means we're taking responsibility for our own actions, and understanding that there are many things such as soul karma, which we aren't able to fully understand with our 3D minds. It means we are being called to radically trust that life knows what it is doing. When we go into fear we block ourselves, cutting ourselves off from divine source. When we trust in life and ourselves we can allow ourselves to be moved by life. If we're still in the muck of it, in the trenches of our soul's growth, it may take some manoeuvring to get us out. It may feel at times like we're going through one inner war after another, as our Higher Self works overtime to get us back on track. If you can just keep that candle of faith burning from within your soul you will find your way back to balance!

EFT example statements for victimisation

"Even though I was attacked by ... and feel like a victim, I now take full responsibility for my life and I am deeply grateful for learning about my boundaries and power."

"Even though I was a victim of sexual abuse, I now take full responsibility for my life, and I claim back my power and am grateful for learning about letting go and my spiritual empowerment."

"Even though I was abused ..., I am deeply grateful for learning about my boundaries, etc."

[Name everything you've learnt from the above experience]

"Even though I am ill and feel like a victim, I now take full responsibility for my life and feel grateful for what this illness is teaching me. I trust in the process of life and that I am exactly where I am meant to be."

[In the above example name all the good things it is teaching you and tap it in. If you really get the learning from the illness, the illness may go.]

"Even though I feel a victim of the system/ or have no money, I now take full responsibility for my life and I am grateful that it is teaching me to step deeper into my own power."

"I now allow myself to trust deeply that I am exactly where I am meant to be."

36

THE DIVINE MASCULINE & FEMININE

If women want to feel honoured by the masculine they need to honour themselves and the masculine. If men want to feel honoured by the feminine, they need to honour themselves and the feminine. Within each and every single one of us there is masculine and feminine energy. When our inner masculine and feminine is out of balance we usually will seek or need it from outside of us in the opposite sex. For instance, if a woman feels she cannot support herself or feel strong within herself when she is by herself she will seek a strong masculine man to help her feel safe by him providing for her, protecting and supporting her on various different levels. If a man is unable to nurture himself he will seek for a woman to nurture him. There is nothing wrong with any of this of course, and most relationships on this planet are co-dependant whether we are in heterosexual relationships or not. However, as we begin to awaken, our soul seeks divine union WITHIN, and if you are really serious about awakening to ALL that you are beyond your conditioning you may need to fly solo for a while. This is not necessarily the case for everyone though. Some souls are blessed to have found soul mates early on who will awaken with their beloveds, but this is rare. When I left my ex-husband I was shown in a dream that I was now to give birth to my own masculine within. It was an incredible opportunity for me to step deeper into my masculine qualities, and even though it was incredibly tough going in the beginning, I am deeply amazed at how I've grown by being on my own. Once we've healed our past and we become whole within by marrying our inner masculine and feminine, we are able to authentically live in the present moment as we live our soul's purpose.

Once we're awakened and fully human we are sovereign and free, and then we may meet someone else romantically who is also sovereign and free. Two whole people who choose to be together for love and service. Within such an empowered relationship there are no more projections, no more demanding expectations, and we are truly free. Of course, we still feel love, sadness, anger, and all of our other feelings, but they arise in the moment and will be cleared out or worked through in the moment rather than being constantly triggered due to past pain. We can still enjoy being held, supported at times, nurtured, and other similar feminine and masculine qualities, but they won't be needed for us to feel whole or safe.

> *When our inner masculine and feminine is out of balance we usually will seek or need it from outside of us in the opposite sex.*

As we cultivate and grow our own inner masculine and feminine into divine union we inevitably become stronger and more independent. There are still qualities we admire and may want to ask for within our romantic relationships, and if it doesn't feel right, we may feel called to leave even an awakened partnership. Here we allow ourselves to be fluid and to respond to our inner needs at all times coming from within our completion and wholeness.

When the divine masculine and feminine marries within, a new journey begins for us spiritually speaking. We are now able to be fully in our divine purpose, serving the earth or humanity with our unique spiritual gifts and talents. It is also true that while we are clearing out the past, and before we are fully integrated and awake, that we are also fulfilling our purpose of awakening and therefore affecting the collective consciousness by allowing ourselves to flower as we heal and raise our spiritual frequency. The process of awakening is a huge part of our soul's purpose! In other words, have compassion for where you are on your journey right now. The quicker you can accept where you are, the easier it is for the energy to move and flow. You are always exactly where you are meant to be, and if it feels wrong or painful, learn what you need to learn so that you can move on.

Healing our mother and father wounds is an essential process in order for us to marry our divine masculine and feminine within. Our mother and father wounding will be continuously brought to us via our present relationships, so you're only to look a little deeper within and around you to see where you still need to heal these wounds. All relationships and challenging situations are bringing you an opportunity for deeper healing, so always look for the gift attached. Sometimes we can only see it years later, and that is totally ok too. Keep the faith in your process of healing that this too shall pass. The law of impermanence guarantees change. Nothing is static; everything is constantly moving and changing in flux and in flow. Trust this flow and allow yourself to drop into this ever-changing movement. Your inner divine union demands radical trust and faith in order to be radically free.

All relationships and challenging situations are bringing you an opportunity for deeper healing, so always look for the gift attached. Sometimes we can only see it years later, and that is totally ok too.

Healing the Mother Wound

Due to the push-down of the feminine for centuries by the controlling patriarchal forces, the mother wound tends to mainly display as a feeling of unworthiness and disempowerment. The way this presents can be as jealousy, feeling less good than and then comparing ourselves to others. It may display as addictions, obsessions, perfectionism, and/or victim mentality. The mother wound is present within men and women. Healing this wound takes time and a lot of inner observation and work. We will keep on attracting the same kind of relationships until we heal our mother or father wounding.

When I was healing my mother wound I kept attracting women into my life that I would look up to, adore and put up on a pedestal. Inevitably they'd always disappoint and often reject me. This is of course exactly what happened with my own mother. This wound kept repeating itself until I healed it. It took many years to heal my mother wound while working on it consciously. My self-esteem was very low when I began to embark on my spiritual journey so it took a lot of reprogramming for me to begin to authentically love and accept myself. I did this with daily EFT, meditation, kinesiology, and various other alternative healing modalities, tools and techniques. We know we've healed this wound when we stop attracting the same scenarios, and when all those needs we have toward the feminine begin to fall away. We know this wound is healed when we can mother ourselves via self-care and self-love. We know it is healed when we don't take other people's stuff so personally, and when we stop giving our power away to others. We simply do not need to take our stuff to our female friends, lovers, wives, mothers or daughters any longer, as we feel complete within. We do not need their unconscious or conscious permission to shine our empowered light within. We know our light and power will never diminish our fellow sisters' light and power, even if they are still trapped in mental programming that are keeping them small.

> *We know we've healed this wound when we stop attracting the same scenarios, and when all those needs we have toward the feminine begin to fall away.*

The final and most powerful healing I ever received on my own mother wounding involved an entire group of people during a week-long silent retreat. During my healing, I was held in a powerful way by the 16 participants while the facilitator held me and told me how much she loved me. She gave to me what I missed during my childhood as I allowed my body to shake while sobbing what felt like all the pain and sadness from my childhood. At the end of my healing the facilitator asked me to sing to them all. As I stepped into my voice and power and sang I felt the healing cementing deeper. I sang the best I've ever sung, and they cheered for a long time. It felt deeply healing allowing myself to be fully received in my vulnerability. I felt a remarkably powerful shift in my consciousness after this healing which allowed for me to start writing this book!

EFT example statements for Mother Wounding

If you work with EFT daily to clear out old patterns related to mother wounding then pay attention to all of your relationships with women, especially the challenging ones. Tap on the emotional triggers within these relationships bringing in for yourself what you need to heal it. For example, if you feel dismissed by women, and if your own mother often dismissed you, you may want to tap the following:

> *"Even though … said … and dismissed me just like my mother did, I unconditionally love, accept, respect and hear myself just as I am."*

Now you can tap on all of your memories where you ever felt dismissed one by one to deeply heal from the ground up.

Remember with tapping the more specific you can be the more powerful the healing will be. Tap on the issue that is triggering you first and foremost, and look at the detail, what you don't want and what you do want. Next tap on your past memories of similar events brining in love, compassion and what it is you need to cement the healing.

To heal is to feel.

A Prayer for Healing the Mother Wound

"Mother Father Divine within, Unconditional Love, I Am Presence,

thank you for giving me your understanding of Divine Feminine qualities so that I can cultivate these within myself. I am deeply grateful for receiving unconditional love and nurture from the Divine Mother within my own being. Thank you for assisting me in healing my mother wounding with unconditional love, self-acceptance and full faith in my spiritual journey. Thank you that I am now able to surrender to my own inner feminine wisdom of effortlessly being so that I can be who I truly am. I love myself deeply on all levels of my being, and I know that I am truly loveable and also divine.

It is done, and so it is. Aho/Amen/Thank You."

Healing the Father Wound

The father wound is the shut-down of our feeling and/or our heart centre, while pushing, forcing and controlling for an outcome. All humans who are still awakening carry both mother and father wounding within. The father wound is the denial of our vulnerabilities and it displays itself as a need to control situations and others. It may appear as coldness or hardness, violence, emotional withdrawal, domination and addiction (the need to escape our true feelings). If your father was emotionally unavailable you most probably will attract men into your life who are emotionally unavailable. To heal the father wound we need to begin to allow ourselves to feel. We must be determined with the unveiling of our inner vulnerabilities.

To heal is to feel. Yes, it is painful, and yes, it is uncomfortable when we're meeting our grief and rage head on, but it is far healthier for us on all levels to feel our trapped emotions away bit by bit, than for them to stay trapped in our physical bodies. We are not wallowing in our stories, or going into the drama when we clear out old stuck

Figure 12: Qualities of the Divine Masculine/Feminine & Father/Mother Wounding

Left Brain   *Right Brain*

Qualities of the Divine Masculine   **Qualities of the Divine Feminine**

Active	Nurturing
Protector	Gentleness
Logical	Creative
Rational	Flowing
Linear	Surrendering
Determined	Flexible
Practical	Peaceful
Goal-oriented	Open minded
Disciplined	Forgiving
Heroic	Understanding
Consistent	Warm
Focused	Soft

Qualities of Father Wounding   **Qualities of Mother Wounding**

Rigid	Manipulative
Stubborn	Weak
Violent	Irrational
Aggressive	Illogical
Domineering	Indecisive
Self-Centred	Fickle
Non-Communicative	Controlling
Closed Minded	Jealousy
Cut off from	Bitchiness
emotions or heart	Powerless
Cynical	Victim
Controlling	Low self-esteem
Blaming others	Overly nice
Irresponsible	Perfectionism

emotions. We are simply allowing ourselves to feel the stored, trapped emotions that we've locked away within the physical body for many years. These trapped emotions can cause physical dis-ease, so when we choose to feel and release these feelings we are actually healing the physical body and prolonging our lives.

We know we have healed the father wound when we are allowing our feelings to flow from moment to moment. We know we've healed this wound when we have pulled ourselves out of our addictions (distractions) and when we begin to accept life as it is. This doesn't mean we become complacent, but rather that we have strengthened our inner trust in life and the Divine. This way we do not need to control the situation or others any longer. We also know we've healed this wound when we take FULL RESPONSIBILITY for our lives and our actions. This wound is healing when we're able to support ourselves and trust ourselves deeply.

We know we have healed the father wound when we are allowing our feelings to flow from moment to moment. We know we've healed this wound when we have pulled ourselves out of our addictions (distractions) and when we begin to accept life as it is.

The father wound also concerns our perception of God the father. Of course, I am referring to the old godhead that is seen as separate from us, the god that punishes and controls. Unfortunately, many of us carry unconscious beliefs around this god that blocks us from being able to trust in the Divine mother father god/goddess within. This ancient religious programming is usually passed down from previous generations and it is deeply embedded within our DNA. You can muscle test yourself to see if you still hold any of the old negative god programming in your unconscious.

Muscle test,

"God is a punishing angry god", or *"I need to suffer in order to spiritually progress".*

I often find these types of beliefs in my clients and have also had to clear these from my own DNA. You can use EFT and prayer to effectively clear out these beliefs from your unconscious. Once you've done the clearing and brought in your newly empowered belief you can muscle test yourself again to see if you still have the belief lodged within the unconscious. It will only stay if on some level it is still serving you, and if that is the case you need to bring in the learning for your soul in order to heal it. It may sound complicated, but it is actually very simple. You can do this work by using your spiritual will and faith.

Once we can fully trust in the Divine, and see life as an extension of ourselves, we are free, knowing that our lives are unfolding in its unique way for our spiritual evolution.

A note on Anger

It is imperative that we begin to create safe space for men and women to express and release their anger and rage. Doing Breathwork with this intention with a drum and possibly by a fire can be life changing and extremely powerful. I envision men's groups where men can be held by men to express in this cathartic way and held in strength, love and compassion by the group. I have held circles like this for women and it is incredibly healing and transformative.

EFT example statements for Father Wounding

"Even though I shouted at/was aggressive/violent … as I felt afraid …, I unconditionally love and accept myself, and trust in the process of my healing journey"

"I now allow myself to feel my feelings and to express these openly with others knowing that it is completely safe for me to do so."

"Even though my father dismissed/abused/beat/ignored me, I unconditionally love and accept myself and trust that I am safe."

"Even though I'm afraid to feel my feelings in case it is too overwhelming,

or in case I'll be judged and ridiculed, I now step deeply into my power and choose to feel my feelings regardless."

"It is safe for me to be vulnerable."

"Even though I've been told that my tears are a weakness, and even though I do cry, I unconditionally love and accept myself and feel the strength within myself as I release the past with my tears."

Often as we heal the mother wound we need to bring in strong divine masculine qualities, and as we heal the father wound we need to meet it with strong divine feminine qualities. We do really need to heal and balance both the feminine and masculine wounding within us to be radically free.

A Prayer for Healing the Father Wound

"Mother Father Divine within, Unconditional Love, I Am Presence,

thank you for assisting me in feeling my feelings, knowing that it is completely safe for me to do so. I am grateful for my ability to express my vulnerabilities to the world, as I meet my inner pain and struggle with love and compassion. I now commit to healing my father wounding and am determined to meet myself emotionally wherever I am. I love myself fully on all levels of my being, and let go of shame and guilt for where I still acted from my unconscious father wounding in the past. Thank you for assisting me in the process of healing these wounds.

It is done, and so it is. Aho/Amen/Thank You."

37

HEALING ANCESTRAL TRAUMA WOUNDING

Much of our pain and life lessons are tied in with our unique ancestral history and wounding. It is what is referred to in the Christian Bible as, *"The sins of the fathers and the mothers."* We carry the gifts and also the pain and trauma of our ancestry within the cells of our bodies. If, for example, someone within our ancestry was raped and/or tortured we will carry a resonance of that trauma, and we may even re-create some of the old ancestral traumas within our lives in the here and now. Luckily, we do not need to put our attention on our ancestry to heal these wounds. We are simply to keep looking ever inwards at what is presenting from within us and in our relationships around us in the present moment to heal it.

You can ask yourself the question, *"Where do I feel blocked or unable to move forward?"*. As we heal these blockages and keep working with our emotional triggers, we'll begin to heal our ancestral wounding. *Boab*, from the Australian Bush Flower Essences range, is a powerful flower remedy that will assist you in clearing out negative ancestral patterning. The Aboriginals knew of the flower's magical properties and birthed their babies while squatting over a hole in the Earth that would be filled with Boab flowers. They believed the flowers helped their babies to clear out negative family patterns and negative karmic ties.

I carried an ancestral blockage around my throat area for most of my life, and even though I am a singer I just couldn't really believe in my talent enough to allow myself to shine. This wound was linked in to an ancestral trauma on my mother's line. Part of healing this wound was also committing to stepping deeper into my power. In other words, I had to step outside of my comfort zone to allow myself to shine on stage. The voice doesn't lie, so I could feel when I sang whether I still felt disempowered and in fear, and when I was able to fully relax into my soul's gift of singing. Tuning in to my voice and how I felt helped me to monitor exactly where I was regarding the healing of this wound.

Everyone on this planet will be born with a unique package of ancestral trauma and wounding within their DNA. We are able to heal these wounds very effectively by continuing our day-to-day inner healing or clearing work on ourselves. Everything we need in order to heal our ancestral wounding will show up for us in the here and now as we continue to heal ourselves.

Everyone on this planet will be born with a unique package of ancestral trauma and wounding within their DNA. We are able to heal these wounds very effectively by continuing our day-to-day inner healing or clearing work on ourselves.

38

HEALING PAST LIFE TRAUMA

We may not need to look for what has happened to us in past lives in order for us to heal past life trauma. From my personal experience if a past life trauma is ready to heal it will usually be shown to you in divine timing. You don't need hypnosis, or to try by pushing or forcing for an answer regarding past lives. If, however, you are synchronistically guided to work with hypnosis to heal a past life trauma then by all means do it.

After my Kundalini awakening I was shown a few traumatic deaths I experienced in my past lives, and I feel it was shown to me for healing at the time and that by witnessing it then I was able to experience the healing. In other words, being shown the memory IS the healing. We simply need to trust that all past life traumas will be healed in time as we keep healing ourselves from within during our day-to-day. We do not need to lose ourselves in past life stories or dramas. This will only act as yet another distraction to the necessary inner work that is required for our authentic awakening.

If a past life trauma is ready to heal it will usually be shown to you in divine timing.

39

THE EGO

The ego is fuelled by disempowerment and the belief and fear that we're not good enough. The ego therefore has to make itself smaller or bigger than others in order to feel separate and alive. The ego thus constantly separates, compares and competes. It wants to feel loved or important, and so will display either as a feeling of feeling sorry for ourselves, or as a feeling of superiority. To heal the ego, we need to begin to heal our self-esteem. EFT is the perfect tool for bringing love and acceptance to this collective wound of not feeling that we're good enough. We are only to look at advertising and marketing campaigns to see how prevalent this ego wounding is on this planet. If we all felt good about ourselves we wouldn't fall for all these adverts that buy into our low self-esteems. When we can observe the ego as low self-esteem and fear it becomes easier to have compassion for it, even in the ugly ways that it can present, such as arrogance. I can't judge intellectual snobbery any longer as I just feel a deep compassion for the ego wounding. Although when I was younger I hated intellectual arrogance. I had a total aversion to it. Understanding the pain of the ego has given me compassion for this type of arrogance.

What also fuels the ego is an addiction to control, which is of course always fear-based. Needing status, and glamour in order to feel powerful or good about ourselves is one of the common side effects of the ego.

The ego is also a false sense of self, a persona or social mask we think is who we are. This mask or persona feels like it is in charge, in control, but underneath its masquerading there are deep-seated fears

such as fear of being out of control, or not being good enough.
The ego is concerned with being in the mind, thought or intellect.
The heart is usually shut down when the ego is in charge. We really
want our hearts to lead, and for our minds to interpret our feeling-
body with clarity and care. You may need to practice moving from
your head to a more heart-based consciousness by placing one hand
on your heart and the other on your belly and asking yourself the
question, how do I feel right now? Then ask yourself how you can
respond to the feeling? Investigate any fears that may arise to block
you from living from your heart. There may be a fear of being judged
or even losing your friends or family. How would it feel to really live
your life from your heart centre honouring yourself and your truth
instead of living your life in fear of how others may perceive you?

*When we can observe the ego as low self-esteem it
becomes easier to have compassion for even in the
ugly ways that it can present, such as arrogance.*

Of course, we cannot live without an ego or personality either. Part
of being a human being here on Earth means that we need an ego to
be able to relate to others, and to survive. But most importantly we
want our ego personality selves to be guided by our loving hearts
instead of fear.

40

ADDICTIONS

The wonders of meditation and EFT and clearing past trauma

When I have clients with addictions I know we will need to do a lot of trauma clearing. Childhood traumas tend to go hand in hand with severe drug addiction for instance. On top of systematically clearing out the traumas we will begin the process of tapping on our presenting addictions too.

Addiction is only a symptom of a deeper issue. Addiction is a checking-out of our day-to-day reality as the pain of our past becomes unbearable. Some won't feel it as emotional pain, as they've shut down to it. They may feel it as boredom, depression or numbness. Some people are addicted to drugs, some to alcohol; some to pornography, gambling, food, social media, even seeking approval can be an addiction that needs to be fed. Of course, some of these addictions are more harmful than others, and some of these addictions can be incredibly harmful towards others. Addiction often has a negative astral component. In other words, there will often be some kind of implant or attachment that will keep the human host in mind control, enslaved to the addiction by spiking the host with thoughts of their addiction. This can make it very difficult to break out of addictive patterning. However, with the right focus and determination coupled with powerful healing techniques and outside support from others we can heal even the toughest addictions.

What can often happen when we break through an addiction is that we shift our relationships that we had when we were still in our addictive patterning. Like attracts like, and you'll most likely feel like a fish out of water for a while as you transition towards more freedom and empowerment. I shifted many friendships when I gave up drugs, alcohol, cigarettes, sugar and wheat addictions. My vibration shifted rapidly and yet for many years I clung on to relationships that gave me no joy or vitality. I didn't realise at the time that for something or someone new to come in to our lives we do actually need to let go of what is dead or dying. If we hang on to the past we aren't making any room for new and fresh energy to enter.

Healing addiction takes time and patience. You need to really want to quit the addiction and this desire needs to be stronger than your desire to still partake in the addiction. Many people want to give up smoking but their desire to smoke is still greater than their desire to quit. Once we have a strong enough desire we still need to work at staying clean. I have found EFT coupled with meditation a brilliant way of clearing out mental addictive patterning. Healing addiction this way will ensure that you do not fall back into old destructive ways. As we raise our energetic frequency, let go of the past and allow for the new to enter, we will eventually be completely free from the old addictions.

Even seeking approval can be an addiction that needs to be fed.

Boronia mixed with *Bottlebrush* from the Australian Bush Essence range assist beautifully in breaking through addictions.

Often when we experience a craving our blood sugars will dip and so supplementing with chromium and liquorice can help us to balance blood sugars and to alleviate cravings. Multi B vitamins and vitamin C can also help to balance the endocrine and may be helpful when we let go of our addictions.

EFT example statements for addiction

"Even though I want to eat as I'm feeling unloved/bored/etc ..., I unconditionally love and accept myself exactly as I am."

[Here you can also tap when you are craving the food or the drug. You can even go so far as to tap with the food, alcohol or drugs right in front of you.]

"Even though I just overate/used drugs/gambled/watched porn/etc, I unconditionally love and accept myself as I am."

"Even though I'm still seeking approval, and did it again earlier when I said ... to ..., I unconditionally love and accept and approve of myself as I am."

And don't forget to tap on ALL of your past traumas!

Finding a new way of being

Finding new daily healthy habits to substitute old addictive patterning can also help us on our way to full recovery. Eating a well-balanced mainly raw diet, filled with highly alkaline foods while doing yoga or some form of daily exercise will definitely help to get the endorphins flowing. Drinking a lot of good quality spring water will help to cleanse the body from old toxicity and spending time in nature can also be incredibly helpful.

I have found EFT coupled with meditation a brilliant way of clearing out mental addictive patterning.

A Prayer for Addiction

"Mother Father Divine within, Unconditional Love, I Am Presence,

Thank you for assisting me in breaking free from the grip of addiction. I now love myself enough to honour my body, my mind and my soul, and to give up and to let go of what no longer serves me. Thank you for helping me focus on self-care and to love myself deeply so that I can find the strength to stay present, grounded and centred. I am deeply grateful for your support on all levels of my being.

It is done, and so it is. Aho/Amen/Thank You."

41

DEPRESSION

"My longing to kill myself, my urge to die to myself, had secretly been my longing to LIVE FULLY, and rest deeply, and slow down, and tell the truth and live and forge ahead with a fragile heart broken open to a sacred Universe."

Jeff Foster[2]

Depression is a shut-down of our emotional body and our power or voice, and therefore we become numb or emotionally shut-down to life. When our emotions are allowed to flow and be expressed we are truly alive, feeling our feelings from moment to moment. As we journey along our awakening path, feeling our feelings may feel overwhelming as we're releasing a lot of pent-up old stuck emotions from the physical and emotional bodies. And yet, if we want to heal from depression it is imperative to break down our heart walls so that we can feel ourselves back to life and freedom again.

Anti-depressants may be necessary to use in extreme cases, but in my opinion, they should not be a long-term solution for depression, as they are not a cure, but rather an artificial suppressant. I know that

---

2 Jeff Foster suffered depression for 20 years prior to his spiritual awakening. Foster, J (2018) Facebook update, 5 May, viewed 5 May 2018, https://www.facebook.com/LifeWithoutA Centre/posts/1590895041008098

when I have clients on my couch with depression who are on anti-depressants, it will be near impossible for them to emotionally break down or through during the session. It is only once they come off anti-depressants that we can begin to do the real deep feeling work required to heal the cause of the depression from the roots up.

Considering how depression is related to the absence of our feelings and a shutting down of our truth I would absolutely suggest Breathwork and Non-Violent Communication (see page 222) one-to-one and also working in groups with others to start the process of expression and feeling.

If you are suffering from depression look to where you are being called to confront others. Taking this simple yet courageous step in confronting those around us with our truth can also pull us out of depression back in to our feeling body, as we begin to engage with life and our feeling body again.

Often with depression there is also a link with Candida over-growth, food intolerances or parasites in the gut, so it would be useful to look into detoxifying. Purifying from heavy metal toxicity may also be incredibly helpful when it comes to healing depression.

Eventually, once you've done enough healing to begin to engage with life again, the dance practice of Five Rhythms and other similar conscious movement practices like Tai Chi, Qi Gong or Yoga can also help to move stagnant or stuck energy from our physical, spiritual, mental and emotional bodies. Similarly, walking in nature may be extremely beneficial too.

Of course, if you are going through a spiritual emergency and say, for instance, you are feeling suicidal, it may be wise to use anti-depressants to tie you over until you can get the deeper more grounded healing your soul needs. You will need to tune in and you'll know when you're ready to wean yourself off. In the meantime, if you are still on anti-depressants please do not beat yourself up about it. Stay in your compassionate heart regarding your mental instability if it is there. Hold yourself through your recovery and make sure you get the support you need to heal deeply and thoroughly. Sometimes we need medical and alternative support alongside each other for a while. After giving birth to my firstborn I was put on 10 different strains of antibiotics, as the doctors couldn't find the right one to heal the unknown infections in my body. I had to surrender to this process even though it was incredibly toxic to my then fragile body. My hands and feet peeled twice in the space of one week! And yet, as soon as I left the hospital I went straight to my Kinesiologist to heal my gut and my broken heart. Sometimes we need alternative and medical solutions alongside each other while keeping the faith in order to move ourselves forward.

Do not come off your anti-depressants without discussing it with your doctor or other health-care practitioners.

Natural solutions for depression

5HTP, St John's Wort, Valerian and multi-B vitamins with extra B5, B6 and B12 may be an excellent alternative to anti-depressants. Also cutting wheat and cow's milk from your diet may be hugely helpful, while detoxing the physical body from Candida, parasitic and heavy metal toxicity. I also highly recommend sunshine, exercise and walking in nature.

EFT example statements for depression

"Even though I feel totally numb to life, I unconditionally love and accept myself as I am, and I step into my power as I open my heart to feeling again, trusting that I am completely safe."

"I now commit to feeling my feelings and expressing my truth regardless of how others respond."

42

LIVING IN THE PRESENT MOMENT

To really live in the present moment, we need to authentically and systematically clear out the past. Clearing out the past involves clearing past traumas, resentments, regrets and guilt. Many teachings tell us to detach from our thoughts or so called 'pain bodies', but if we detach prematurely without investigating and healing the original pain or trauma then we cannot awaken authentically. The only way to authentic presence and radical freedom would be to clear the past by meeting it with unconditional love, acceptance and forgiveness as we investigate our thoughts and feelings with compassion.

Many teachings tell us to detach from our thoughts or so called 'pain bodies', but if we detach prematurely without investigating and healing the original pain or trauma then we cannot awaken authentically.

Once you make the decision to awaken in this life, your Higher Self will begin to set things in motion via challenges you'll need to face in order to let go of the past and grow in strength and spiritual empowerment. It is natural and easy for us to live in presence when we have forgiven our past, and learn to deal with our daily stress through self-care and rest. But it takes time for us to authentically be present. Unfortunately, many of these oneness, presence or non-dual teachings can actually cause more stress to the student than relief, as they tend to struggle to detach or not think of the past or the future. When we resist our thoughts they'll keep coming regardless, yet now we're in resistance or denial rather than staying in open curiosity and investigation. If only we could be more kind to ourselves and compassionately observe our thinking instead. It is important not to judge yourself when your mind does go to the past or future, as it usually will point you to a much-needed healing that needs to happen for you to be free from that particular thought.

Meditation teaches presence, and when we meditate we are invited not to force our mind into submission by rejecting our thoughts. We simply observe the mind and bring it back to the breath or the body. When you meditate in this surrendered way you'll begin to clear out mental blockages and limiting belief patterns too. It will also teach your mind how to be totally ok with what is going on in your mind and also in your external reality. And by being totally ok with your thoughts, you'll begin to cultivate presence for exactly what is here and now. The important thing here to remember is not to struggle, grasp or push for anything to happen.

Living in the present moment should never be used as an excuse not to do our inner shadow work. Authentically completing our shadow work tends to precede being authentically present.

43

COMMON LIMITING BELIEFS WITH EXAMPLE STATEMENTS AND PRAYERS

Below follow some limiting beliefs and fears most humans hold within their unconscious. They take time and practice to deeply and authentically root out:

1. "I'm not good enough" and the fear of not being good enough

"I'm not good enough" or *"I'm afraid of not being good enough"* is really what creates and feeds the ego (the separate self), and this is the belief that keeps humanity disempowered and enslaved in victim consciousness. Because we feel no good about ourselves we then begin to place ourselves either below or above others. It essentially is also part of the Mother Wound, which of course is present in both men and women. This belief of not feeling good enough drives us to seek approval from others, and so we constantly give our power away to others by unconsciously or consciously asking for their permission for us to do what we really want to do, or to do what we think may impress them, rather than what is an authentic expression within ourselves.

In my experience, it takes time and practice to thoroughly clear out this program and fear. We'll need to be patient as we keep spiralling inwards towards our soul's sovereignty and emancipation. I tapped on every single past memory that made me feel I wasn't good enough and brought in self-love and acceptance. I also tapped on issues related to my current relationships every time this wound was triggered to clear it out thoroughly and deeply. It took me many years to unravel this belief program as it is incredibly deeply ingrained not only through the ancestry, but as it is also prevalent in our culture, and almost everywhere we look (media/advertising for example).

The belief that we're not good enough may display as depression and/or addiction, *"I'm no good so I may as well check out, numb myself down or try to cover this pain with self-harming addictive behaviours."*

EFT example statements for not feeling good enough

"Even though I don't feel good enough because of ..., I unconditionally love and accept myself just as I am, and trust that I am safe."

"Even though my mother/father said she hated me when I was 13 [and think of the specific memory], *and I just don't feel good enough, I unconditionally love and accept myself just as I am."*

"Even though ... looked at me in a weird way today when I said ... and it made me feel not good enough, I unconditionally love and accept myself just as I am, and I trust in my lovability."

The fear of not being good enough is as deep an issue as the feeling of not being good enough, and displays as perfectionism and approval seeking. In other words, we feel we have to do everything perfectly in order to be good enough. The fear of not being good enough may begin to serve us in this way, where we have to strive or do things in order to gain approval or love from others. To heal this fear we need to teach our conscious and unconscious selves that we can be loved for exactly who we are. Meditation alongside EFT may also really assist us in dissolving this fear, but it will take time to dismantle as with the belief of not feeling good enough.

Below are some further examples of tapping on the fear of not being good enough:

"Even though this specific thing happened and I'm really afraid I'm not good enough, I unconditionally love and accept myself just as I am regardless of how others respond, and I trust in my lovability."

"Even though ... judged me and rejected me for not being good enough, I love and accept myself and I shine my light regardless."

And don't forget to tap on your daily triggers. If, for example, someone triggers this wound of not being good enough you can tap on the immediate trigger and add in that you don't feel or that you're afraid of not being good enough. For instance, if a friend fails to invite you along on holiday but invites some of your other mutual friends, and you're left feeling really hurt, rejected and not good enough you'll tap,

"Even though ... didn't invite me along on holiday and yet ... was invited and I don't feel good enough, I unconditionally love and accept myself exactly as I am"

By bringing the light of love and acceptance to this wound you'll begin to dissolve it as you move along your path to inner freedom.

A Prayer for Not Feeling Good Enough

"Mother Father Divine within, Unconditional Love, I Am Presence,

thank you for assisting me in loving and accepting myself fully. I am deeply grateful that I now know on all aspects of my being that it is possible for me too, and that I am healing this fear and belief of not being good enough. Thank you for guiding me with synchronicity to unconditional love and acceptance of all of myself, including my shadow and my fears. I love and accept myself on all levels of my being.

It is done, and so it is. Aho/Amen/Thank You."

We'll need to be patient as we keep spiralling inwards towards our soul's sovereignty and emancipation.

2.   "I'm afraid of my power"

The fear of our own power keeps us small, as we tend to feel afraid of what may happen if we step into our power. We also seem to hold within old unconscious negative and limiting belief programs around power, as we've seen or experienced the dark side of power over others (the masculine or father wound). We need to teach ourselves, and our unconscious minds that it is safe for us to step deeply into our spiritual power. This can take time, especially when we have ancestral and often past life traumas related to power. False light programming that relates to always being nice and good at the expense of your own truth will also keep you disempowered and enslaved, and it takes time to break free from this deeply embedded programming. This fear will display as keeping small or having to hide in order to be safe.

We need to teach ourselves, and our unconscious minds that it is safe for us to step deeply into our spiritual power.

Negative power vs. Spiritual Empowerment

Negative power is to have power over others. This type of power can become highly addictive like a drug and relates to greed, ego and service to SELF, even if it hurts others. A good example of this negative power would be to look at companies who are only focused on earning profits, rather than whether their products are actually good for their consumers or the Earth. The founder of Nestle was quoted saying that water shouldn't be a human right for example. It would serve the founder to monopolise water as he would get more power (profits), but of course it would be disastrous for human beings and the planet.

Spiritual Empowerment simply means we love ourselves fully and won't give our energy or power away to anyone else. We will not allow ourselves to be manipulated or controlled in any way. It means we take full responsibility for our lives and are sovereign and free. It relates to service to OTHERS as we are fully empowered and can thus begin to serve humanity and the planet. Healing our selves, and self-care are also service to others. As we heal ourselves we're assisting the collective to awaken. Essentially, we can't heal others. We can only heal ourselves and show others how to heal themselves.

EFT example statements for the fear of power

Here you can tap the following example statements:

"I now trust that it is safe for me to be in my full spiritual power, as I trust in the process of life and I trust in myself and the Divine."

"Even though my power may cause others to judge or reject me, I unconditionally love and accept myself and shine my powerful light regardless"

"Even though I am overpowering others and dominate and control my children, I unconditionally love and accept myself, and I trust that I can change this pattern of behaviour knowing that I am fully supported by the Divine."

"I now trust that it is safe for me to trust in the flow of life and death. I let go knowing that I am safe and supported by the Divine."

Spiritual Empowerment simply means we love ourselves fully and won't give our energy or power away to anyone else.

A Prayer for Empowerment

"Mother Father Divine within, Unconditional Love, I Am Presence,

thank you for assisting me in stepping deeper into my power and strength. I trust with every cell, part and aspect in my being, that it is safe for me to be powerful. I let go of and release all past life, ancestral and this lifetime traumas related to the misuse of power where others had power over me, used me for their own ends, or where I may have done the same to others. Thank you for giving me your divine understanding of spiritual empowerment, and that I can safely live my life without giving my power away to others. I am deeply grateful for my own inner strength and my ability to step fully into my spiritual power. Thank you for assisting me in letting go of the past and to authentic forgiveness and keeping the faith so that I can shine my soul light in its glorious empowerment.

It is done and so it is. Aho/Amen/Thank You."

3. "I'm afraid of being out of control"

Of course during trauma we are usually out of control, and this can feel very scary indeed. Our unconscious minds work hard to keep us safe, and so this fear will usually attract towards us, as all fear does, exactly that which we're afraid of in order for us to free ourselves from this fear. This fear wants us to learn how to trust in a deeper more profound way. It brings to us the opportunity to trust in ourselves, life and the divine, so that even when things do get unstable or out of control that we can remain calm knowing that there is a greater learning or gift attached. Cultivating a deep trust in the divine will clear out this unconscious fear and help us along our path toward radical freedom.

The truth is that we are out of control, and that the only thing we can control is how we respond to life. Life just happens. Vipassana meditation teaches us to stay equanimeous regardless of what happens. Everything is subject to change, and even the sun will eventually die. Nothing stays the same. Nothing is permanent except for impermanence. Meditation thus instils in us a deep peace, faith and trust in ourselves, life and the divine.

EFT example statements for feeling out of control

"Even though I am completely out of control, I trust that I am safe, I trust myself, life and the divine."

"Even though I'm terrified of being out of control, and so I eat/take drugs/go on Facebook, etc, I unconditionally love and accept myself as I am and trust in the process of life."

I also recommend that you tap through all of your past memories where you felt unsafe and out of control and tap in trust, faith and safety.

"Even though … happened and I was completely out of control, I now trust that I am completely safe, I trust myself, life and the divine."

The truth is that we are out of control, and that the only thing we can control is how we respond to life. Life just happens.

A Prayer for the Fear of Being Out of Control

"Mother Father Divine within, Unconditional Love, I Am Presence,

thank you for assisting me in healing all of my past memories where I felt out of control and unsafe. Thank you for strengthening my faith and trust in YOUR way, so that I can get out of the way to allow for your love to bring healing and strength into my life. I now connect in with my inner warrior energy as I shine my faith in my path, in life and myself outwards. I fully connect with your divine way by allowing myself to be lifted out of fear into love and safety. Thank you for your full support in this.

It is done, and so it is. Amen/Aho/Thank You."

4.   "I'm rejected" or afraid of rejection

When we feel rejected, we'll keep attracting rejection into our lives. The only way to heal this belief and this fear is to begin the process of deeply and unconditionally loving and accepting ourselves fully. Once we do love ourselves fully we'll stop attracting rejection, and if someone then does reject us we'll understand that it isn't personal, while at the same time trusting that it is for our highest and best not to be in that particular relationship.

EFT example statements for rejection

"Even though they've rejected me, I unconditionally love and accept myself just as I am, and I shine my light regardless."

"Even though I'm really afraid of being rejected tomorrow when I have to do my public speech, I unconditionally love and accept myself and my feelings, and I trust that I am safe."

[Tap on all of your past memories where you were or felt rejected and bring in love and acceptance for yourself. This way you will slowly, slowly begin to heal this wound.]

A Prayer for Rejection

"Mother Father Divine within, Unconditional Love, I Am Presence,

thank you for helping me heal the soul wounds within my past lives, ancestry and this lifetime where I was or felt rejected by others. I now open myself up to receiving your unconditional love and acceptance for where I felt rejected in the past, and where I then began rejecting myself. I am deeply grateful that this inner and outer rejection has taught me to be more compassionate, more loving and forgiving towards others and myself. I now choose to love and accept all of my shadow, my fears and myself as I allow myself to awaken with ease and grace.

It is done, and so it is. Amen/Aho/Thank You."

---

5. "I'm abandoned" or afraid of abandonment

Similar to the belief and fear of rejection, abandonment seems to be another deeply embedded unconscious block for most people. There may have been an obvious abandonment from a parent, or perhaps even being born into this imperfect world and not being given a conscious awareness of where we're from or where we are going, may feel like an abandonment from the Divine. I felt abandoned by the Universe for many years as I could not understand how a loving God or Goddess would allow so much suffering on this planet and within our lives. How could it be allowed that I suffered sexual abuse from my maternal grandfather at such a tender young age over and over again? My trust in the divine felt broken and my place in this world felt unsafe. It took me many years of deep healing to begin the process of trusting my path and the Divine. Part of this process was experientially discovering that the Divine was truly within me, rather than a separate angry punishing god outside of myself. Understanding that god/goddess was within me helped me to take responsibility for my life and to step deeper into my empowerment.

A large part of healing this fear of abandonment from the divine is thus healing our past traumas, and bringing in trust and safety.

Of course, along this road of stepping deeper into my empowerment I also systematically attracted all of my unconscious fears so that my soul would be able to work through these to radically free myself from fear's grip. During this process, it can feel daunting as we face one intense fear after another. I went through phases where I would wake at 3am in total terror, and I'd get myself out of bed, and start pacing the floor while tapping directly on the fear I was feeling. This process felt incredibly testing at the time, and it gave me a deeper understanding of why people do commit suicide. When we're in terror or fear we block ourselves from receiving the love and safety from the Divine that is of course always available to us. It takes time and patience to clear this fear and to bring in faith and trust in the Divine, and ourselves but it is a worthy cause to work towards, as your soul's eternal freedom will be the reward.

When we are in fear we are abandoning the Divine.

When we are in fear we are abandoning the Divine, which is expressed as unconditional love and trust within. Our fears often create themselves, so in other words when you're in fear of being abandoned by the Divine, you're abandoning yourself and the Divine.

Before my Kundalini awakening I always tried to avoid rejection, abandonment and judgement. I now look forward to meeting this energy as I witness my inner response to see whether I need any further healing on my self-esteem and boundaries. Meeting judgement and rejection from others openly will give us the inner strength and courage we need to break the spell of our disempowerment.

Sometimes we can feel rejected or abandoned by another, and that rejection may be based on an assumption. We then close down our hearts and reject that person, becoming exactly what hurt us so much in the first place. And then we may find out that the other person was going through a divorce or a difficult time, and that their withdrawal of their energy wasn't personal at all. How much can we lose when we express our vulnerabilities with others? Being openly vulnerable IS our strength! This is not about being right or wrong, but simply being willing to put our feelings out there so that we can then act according to the truth rather than acting on an assumption that was made inside our heads. If that person admits that they were consciously rejecting you, wouldn't you rather know that truth than having to guess? You can then draw a line underneath that relationship and move forward freely. Loving yourself fully will mean that you'll confront this type of energy head on. This way you know who and what is good for you and what isn't.

EFT example statements for abandonment

> *"Even though I was abandoned by ..., I unconditionally love and accept myself and trust that I am safe."*

> *"Even though I am afraid of being abandoned by ..., I unconditionally love and accept myself knowing that I am safe."*

> *"Even though I went through this trauma ..., I unconditionally love and accept myself and trust in myself, life and the Divine."*

[Here you can tap on all of your specific traumas where you felt truly abandoned by the Divine]

> **A Prayer for the Fear of Abandonment**
>
> "Mother Father Divine within, Unconditional Love, I Am Presence,
>
> I now allow your unconditional love, abundance and support to envelop me as I choose to meet myself where I have felt or where I still feel abandoned, rejected, judged or not good enough. I commit to bringing the light of love, acceptance and compassion to these abandoned, judged, rejected and low self-esteem parts of my being. Thank you for keeping me focused on this inner work so that I may love myself back to wholeness. I trust in the process of awakening. I trust myself. I trust in life and I trust in the Divine.
>
> It is done, and so it is. Aho/Amen/Thank You."

6.   "I'm a failure" or fear of failure

Most people are so afraid of failure that they block their entire life and soul's purpose! Fear of failure is usually tied in with the fear of judgement and rejection. Ask yourself what the worst thing would be if you failed? The Beatles failed over 20 times as they tried to get a record deal. We must get in to the idea of failure. Failure is an opportunity and a necessity for growth and learning. When you trust life, the Divine and yourself it is truly impossible to fail, as any perceived failure would be seen as an opportunity for soul expansion or growth. Life is messy and filled with failures and mistakes for all of us. Let's begin to look forward to these, celebrating our growth and our faith in the process of life!

Life is messy and filled with failures and mistakes for all of us. Let's begin to look forward to these, celebrating our growth and our faith in the process of life!

EFT example statement for fear of failure

"Even though I failed when I lost the ..., I unconditionally love and accept myself as I am, and I trust in the process of life."

"Even though I am afraid of failing with this project, I unconditionally love and accept myself and my feelings, as I trust in the process of life and my spiritual path."

A Prayer for the Fear of Failure

"Mother Father Divine within, Unconditional Love, I Am Presence,

thank you for strengthening my faith and trust in all that I am experiencing. Thank you for showing me that my failures are a part of my successes and spiritual learnings. Thank you for brining me inner forgiveness and a deeper understanding of my spiritual path on all levels of my being. I trust that my perceived failures are powerful opportunities for me to step deeper within my spiritual empowerment, and I feel deeply grateful for this process of soul learning.

It is done, and so it is. Aho/Amen/Thank You."

44

NEW AGE OR SPIRITUAL MYTHS, FALSE LIGHT & BYPASSING

Spiritual bypassing or what I like to call 'false light' is a term that is used to describe when we jump to the light, enlightenment or the spiritual before we've done the necessary shadow work to authentically free ourselves. In other words, we fake our bliss and light while hiding our shame and fears. I was a spiritual bypasser for many years before my Kundalini awakening, and looking back on it now I can see that I was desperately wanting to do the right thing, be the light, and that I just did not know any better at the time. I was in denial of my shadow as I believed wholeheartedly that I should only focus my energy on the light. After all I didn't want to attract anything dark, and according to most New Age spiritual teachings I was taught that if I wanted love and light in my life I was to keep my focus on love and light only. So, I bypassed my shadow/shame and jumped prematurely to 'enlightenment'. If you have been bypassing too, don't beat yourself up about it, as it usually comes from a well-meaning place within you. Also, you can trust that your soul will always make a course correction if you've gone off track into bypassing, so eventually you'll be shown the truth of where you've suppressed or been hiding out, and then you'll have to dig deep to heal authentically from the ground up. This is of course exactly what happened to me.

You can trust that your soul will always have to make a course correction if you've gone off track into bypassing, so eventually you'll be shown the truth of where you've suppressed or been hiding out.

Most people within religious structures like Christianity, Catholicism or Islam also bypass or are trapped within false light ideologies. I used to witness this first hand when my mother would sing her Christian songs during church services with huge smiles and hands in the air worshipping, and yet behind closed doors would be emotionally abusive. I remember even then thinking to myself that I never ever wanted to be like that. It drove me to seek the true light of my authentic soul's essence. I've witnessed this exact type of false light bypassing in New Age Ayahuasca gatherings, where everyone is gathering in love and light, sing spiritual songs and mantras and then once the events are done they go back to their day-to-day lives with no tangible daily self-clearing protocol. They expect the psychoactive plant to do the work for them, just as many Christians expect Jesus to do the work for them. The truth is that we are the only ones who can save ourselves by taking full responsibility for our lives and doing the inner daily work required for our healing.

The truth is that we are the only ones who can save ourselves by taking full responsibility for our lives and doing the inner daily work required for our healing.

I've seen many people get completely trapped within these religious false light structures. I'm not judging the Ayahuasca plant or Jesus here. I am looking here at how people distort the truth and how they remain in victim consciousness by expecting something outside of themselves to do the work for them. Ultimately a plant or a teacher can point us to a deeper place of understanding or awareness, but it is our job to do the inner work required to authentically awaken by purifying ourselves on all levels of our being. This is the only true way to inner radical freedom.

Examples of Spiritual Bypassing/False Light/ Spiritual Denial

Fake forgiveness

Saying we've forgiven someone, but actually inside we're still hiding our resentment, rage and anger, due to shame and inner judgement, is an example of spiritually bypassing. We may genuinely want to forgive, and then we think we should forgive to be spiritual or that it is bad to feel anger or resentment, so then we say (pretend) we've forgiven but inside we're fuming. Of course, we don't have to become friends with people we forgive, and often we do naturally move on to different relationships, but when you genuinely forgive someone, unless you knew they wanted to harm you, it wouldn't be a big deal if you ran into them in the street. If, for instance, your opponent never owned their wrongdoing it is perfectly ok not to greet or hug them. This can be a form of fierce love where you honour your boundaries and truth, but you'll need to make sure you're responding from fierce love and not resentment as you stand in your spiritual empowerment. When your thoughts are still a little all over the place concerning the other party, thinking about what happened and how they treated you, etc, then you haven't worked through it properly yet. ESR, EFT and meditation can speed up authentic forgiveness, but even with these incredibly powerful tools, it still tends to take time, practice and patience especially during the process of awakening from unconsciousness to consciousness. The more we can honour ourselves and others as we move through our darker emotions on our journey to forgiveness and spiritual empowerment, the easier and more healing and enlightening for everyone around us. When we shame ourselves or others for feeling victimised, angry, sad, resentful, etc, it can often block the energy of authentic forgiveness and empowerment.

"Turn the other cheek"

Turn the other cheek is a common Christian false light belief program instilled within the collective consciousness, specifically to disempower, victimise and enslave human beings. If we are to turn the cheek in the face of a domineering bully they may just continue to bully and harm us. We MUST learn to stand up for ourselves, to speak out and to say NO, go away, leave me alone or even fuck off if the penny still hasn't dropped. This does not make you a bad person!! Darkness and distorted energy on this planet wants you to believe that you being in your power and in your boundaries is a bad thing, and a thing to feel shame or guilt over. If someone slaps you, you have every right to push him or her back and to say no. Then by all means walk away and keep yourself away from that harmful energy. False light wants human beings to be open and accepting of dark unconscious energy. False light wants you to be confused, coercing with the unconscious darkness in your confusion, and by giving your power and boundaries away.

"You are projecting/It is your projection/Everyone projects onto me"

I see and hear these phrases all the time being used as a way to deny looking within and taking responsibility. Yes, it is true, we often project. But it is also true that we do not always project. And sometimes we project and even though we're projecting the other person or party also has a wound that needs to be owned in order to heal.

"We are all One"

"We are all one" or *"you are pure awareness"*, *"just be present"* are further examples of spiritual bypasses I see thrown around a lot. This tends to go hand in hand with the *"you are not your story"* bypass. It is true on one level that we are one and that we are not our stories, but at the same time we are here on Earth having a human experience working through our day-to-day lessons in order to grow. Our stories are an essential part of our healing, and when we deny our stories, our wounds and pain we are denying our opportunity for deep soul healing. If we were all one and it was all perfect, then why

are we evolving at all? Yes, we need to accept where we are right now, and where we are is always perfect, but within this perfection we are evolving and growing spiritually. We do need determination and to do the inner work in order to expand and ground into our awakening. Do not become complacent thinking that there is nothing to heal! This is a classic New Age spiritual bypass.

Of course, it is beneficial for us to surrender, to trust and to let go, but if you are in touch and in tune with your natural soul's rhythms and timing you will be shown how to balance surrendering and letting go with determination and hard work. And you'll be shown how to surrender in to determination when needed. Meditation teaches this balance beautifully. It is our job to intuit and discern when to surrender and when to be actively doing the work. And remember our mistakes and failures are always signs of growth, as we are given opportunity for re-evaluation and change.

We do need determination and to do the inner work in order to expand and ground into our awakening. Do not become complacent thinking that there is nothing to heal!

"Everything happens for a reason"

"*Everything happens for a reason*" is a phrase that can be used to deny someone else's or your own pain, rage, anger or grief. It can feel incredibly harsh and uncompassionate if, for example, someone has terminal cancer and someone pipes up that "*everything happens for a reason*". Yes, it is true that we are in a Universe where we are always brought an opportunity to learn from our pain and suffering, and where we can turn our anguish into forgiveness, faith and trust if we choose to heal it. But even in the healing there is a process that often takes years for us to authentically move through in order to free ourselves from the pain and suffering of what had occurred. Maybe ask yourself what would be the most compassionate thing to say right now? Or don't say anything at all and just be presence and acceptance for them or yourself.

"It is their karma"

Using the phrase *"It is their karma"* can be used to avoid taking responsibility and assisting others when we're able to. It is true that there is a law of karma in this Universe and that energy will keep bouncing back until we learn our lessons, but most of this is operating at a deeply unconscious level. If only we can be more forgiving and compassionate with others and ourselves as we all make mistakes, especially when we're still working through our layers of unconsciousness. The more we work through our own shadow wounding and karma the more naturally we'll be compassionate when we see others within their own karmic wounding and healing. There is certainly no need to point out someone's karma when they're in the midst of turmoil. We are all working through our own karma and it is challenging all of us here on this planet.

"No judgements"

"No judgements" can also be used to bypass or deny our true feelings. We want to live in no judgement as we've heard it is spiritual, and so when judgement arise within we push it down and pretend it isn't there. To heal this bypass we need to admit our inner judgements to ourselves so that we can begin the process of healing these. And remember that we usually project our inner judgement outwards onto others. There is also a difference between judgements and being discerning. Sometimes we need to look at a situation from many different angles in order to discern whether it is right for us. Your discernment will strengthen as you learn from your previous mistakes and failures. We need to learn to listen to our gut and our hearts, and to then allow for our minds to be the interpreter of our inner feelings. All of this will help us to make better choices in life. Stop shaming and judging yourself and others, and work through your judgements with EFT or meditation instead.

"Focus on the light"

"Be positive and focus only on the light", and *"it is all good"*, can be yet another spiritual bypass as we may be ignoring some inner mud that needs to be shifted through in order to authentically come to our inner light. Of course, it is important to focus our attention on the

light and on solutions, as what we focus our attention on does influence us and tend to grow, but we shouldn't do it at the expense of hiding or denying our shadow. If we can focus our energy on the light and also simultaneously do our inner shadow work, then we are using the law of attraction in a way that is conducive to our spiritual growth. We are invited to go inwards diving into the depths of our shadows bringing love and compassion to these rejected emotions and parts in order for these to heal. This is again a process that can take many years or lifetimes to complete. Also, when we dive into the shadow we are not doing this to wallow or endlessly process either. We are simply bringing our light and love to these wounded rejected shadowy parts within.

"There is no right or wrong"

"There is no right or wrong" is another New Age phrase that I hear and read often. Oh, how false light (the dark/unconsciousness) thrives when human beings are confused! The truth is that there is right and wrong doing. Deliberately harming others is wrongful action, unless of course you're being threatened in the moment and you're defending yourself! And I would say that treating others as we would like for others to treat us is to act from a place of rightful action. Imagine if we tell our children that there is no right or wrong. They'd have no boundaries, and most probably would feel unsafe. Knowing what is right and wrong for you, and where your limitations are, are sure signs of having healthy spiritual boundaries.

"There is no such thing as Truth"

The truth is what is, exactly as it is, without it being interpreted. Any interpretation of the truth is an interpretation of the truth. An opinion of that interpretation is an opinion, and not the truth. I have always been a lover of truth, and a truth seeker my entire life. I thrive on truth. All this searching and seeking to finally discover that the truth just is what it is. There is nothing we can do about it as it just is. How wonderfully freeing! This means we can trust and let go knowing that the truth shall well and truly set us free. But, there are many truths hidden from humans, and as we awaken along our path to radical freedom we may feel shocked to discover some of these. In any case, this is how it unfolded for me. I had no idea of this false reality matrix here on Earth for example. I was so deeply mesmerised by the dream of this 3D reality system that I believed it was real. But as we travel deeper and deeper within our multi-dimensionality we will be shown deeper and deeper layers of truth.

"There is no such thing as truth" is exactly what false light teachings want you to believe, keeping you in confusion, and in the dark. Become a lover of truth and stand firm within it. The wonderful thing about truth is that it doesn't matter whether people argue about it as it won't change the truth.

Also, when you tune in to the truth of your own feelings only you know how you are feeling. No one else can tell you how you're feeling. Stand in the truth of your feelings always and you will quickly attract your soul's tribe rather than wasting your time with people you're trying to impress. Living authentically is about living your own truth.

45

MANIFESTATION, INTENTION & THE LAW OF ATTRACTION

Allow yourself to be manifested via the Divine rather than manifesting from your separate sense of self.

The law of attraction is one of our many laws that exist within our vast multi-dual Universe. Like seems to attract like, and I do experience this daily and can see how I've evolved over the last 20 years of my life and with that how my relationships have reflected me along the way.

Pushing and forcing for an outcome always comes from a place of fear and control, whereas aligning with our joy, our purpose, gratitude and solutions we may want to create comes from a place of surrender and trust.

Pushing and forcing for an outcome always comes from a place of fear and control, whereas aligning with our joy, our purpose, gratitude and solutions we may want to create comes from a place of surrender and trust. It is a very different energy. Personally, I'd throw out the vision boards and stop trying to manifest my perfect soul mate or job, and I'd focus my energy on feeling grateful in the here and now.

Do what you love

You may want to ask yourself, what is it that I can do right now that will open or bring joy to my heart? You can't go too far off your soul's purpose and path if you're doing what you absolutely love. The energy of following your joy and love is stronger than any vision board will ever be. You're also giving the Universe an opportunity to step in and to work its magic, and to turn your desire into something even more incredible than what you may have thought of in your head in the first place. The energy of unconditional love that is beyond duality can bring miracles into our lives, but it is about aligning with it by purifying yourself mentally, physically, emotionally and spiritually. You can then be a clear vessel for your soul's essence to flow freely in divine synchronicity. You wouldn't need to manifest or even intend, as you're just in the stream of your soul's purpose, radically free to be YOU. So yes, focus your energy on the light, but not at the expense of any inner darkness you still need to accept and forgive within yourself. Dive into these darker places with your soul light of unconditional love, acceptance and forgiveness, keep your focus on the solutions, and you'll heal faster than you can imagine.

What is it that I can do right now that will open or bring joy to my heart? You can't go too far off your soul's purpose and path if you're doing what you absolutely love. The energy of following your joy and love is stronger than any vision board will ever be.

When we stretch in yoga we may feel uncomfortable or challenged as we allow ourselves to deeply drop or surrender into our posture. If we push or force a yoga stretch we may cause an injury to our physical bodies. It is the same in life, and that we can allow ourselves to surrender into places where we may feel challenge, as this is where our ability to grow will lie. Allowing ourselves to be challenged in order to grow, where for instance we feel our fear and we do it anyway, i.e. bravery, determination or courage, is a very different energy to pushing or forcing. I love to surrender into determination when my soul is guided me in this particular way.

Ultimately, once we've remove all of our fear and mental blockages we'll find ourselves in our natural state where we are ALWAYS abundant flowing with our creativity, doing what we love.

Gratitude

When we truly align with the energy of gratitude we are automatically in full faith and trust, love and peace. The feeling of gratitude is one of the highest vibrational frequencies we have on this planet! Feeling authentic gratitude from deep within our hearts can clear negative energetic attachments faster than almost anything else can! Gratitude will also align you with more of what you're feeling grateful for. Gratitude is faith on top of joy and abundance.

Abundance

A wise friend told me that abundance is always having what we truly need in the moment. In other words when you've aligned to the flow of abundance what you need will show up synchronistically as you need it. To be in the flow of your natural abundant state you will automatically be in faith and gratitude expressing your soul's essence from moment to moment.

46

TRIGGERING AND PROJECTION

Meeting our emotional triggers as opportunities for growth and freedom

I highly recommend tapping on your daily triggers as part of your self-healing daily protocol. During my own journey of awakening I began to work on my daily emotional triggers with EFT. Every time I felt emotionally triggered by something or someone I'd tap on it that same evening.

An emotional trigger can be a feeling of upset, resentment or pain due to something someone else did or said. After doing daily work on my emotional triggers I began to feel fewer and fewer triggers. Nowadays I very rarely get triggered emotionally, and feel grateful when I do, as it brings me an opportunity for deeper healing and clearing.

As we clear our triggers we're able to better tune into the truth of our relationships to others. Clearing our triggers means we won't take anything personally any longer. It is one of the most powerful boundaries we can assert. How can someone bully you if you don't take what they say personally? It would be impossible, and they'd get bored very quickly and rather move on to bullying the person who'll get emotionally hurt and take it personally.

Also, once you begin to clear through your daily triggers you'll automatically begin to work on your communication skills so that you can deal with triggers in a more diplomatic, effective and enlightened way. When we're able to communicate our feelings, our needs and our boundaries effectively we will avoid feelings of resentment.

EFT example statements for triggering

To tap on your triggers you need to ask yourself why you felt triggered in the first place. How did what the other person said or did make you feel? Then ask yourself how you'd like to feel. For instance, if you felt judged by the other person for being ignorant and you want to feel honoured and respected for who you are, you would tap the following,

> *"Even though I was judged for being ignorant today, I unconditionally love, respect and accept myself as I am."*

You can also tap the following after this initial tap,

> *"Even though I am ignorant, I unconditionally love, accept, respect and honour myself as I am."*

This way, if for any reason, your unconscious mind is still judging yourself for being ignorant, you can now heal this judgement by bringing in love and acceptance for yourself. The amazing thing is that when you truly accept and love yourself including your own ignorance, you'd stop attracting people into your life who would also judge you for being ignorant. How can anyone judge you for it when you don't feel it inside, and if they did, it would be impossible to take them seriously or to take it personally, as you'd be totally ok with it. You'd know that the judgement was a reflection of them (a true projection), and that it had nothing to do with you. A trigger may not be as obvious as someone judging you, and it may just be a feeling that arises within that will point you to an emotional/mental imbalance. Always ask the question how it is making you feel, and then tap on that feeling in you by bringing love and acceptance to it.

Clearing your daily emotional triggers with EFT will be one of the fastest ways to heal your shadow, strengthen your boundaries and step into your spiritual empowerment. It is phenomenally powerful to work with EFT in this way as we watch our triggers melt away into a deep acceptance and forgiveness.

A trigger may not be as obvious as someone judging you, and it may just be a feeling that arises within that will point you to an emotional/ mental imbalance.

Projections (a deeper understanding)

If you can see that someone is genuinely projecting his or her stuff and that it truly has nothing to do with you, then you'd most probably feel compassion for that person. You'd see that they're in pain, and you'd be able to explain to them that it really wasn't about you at all. Of course, not every situation is black and white, and each and every situation will call for us to respond in a unique way, but if you're triggered by someone else's so-called projection of you, then you need to look deeper within yourself to heal your own wounding that caused the pain or resentment in the first place. It takes a lot of courage and strength to look at yourself honestly in this way, but it is an essential part of our inner work on our way to becoming radically free.

For instance, if you frequently feel unheard or unseen, you'll keep attracting this into your life. Let's say one of your closest friends is having a conversation with you and some other friends, and for some reason your friend is not making eye contact with you. Maybe your friend knows you're there, and feels confident enough in your company to not always look at you. But, because of your wounding you may now feel a resentment and pain begin to build. *"He didn't look at me. He didn't acknowledge me. Not even once."* All these thoughts will begin to build in your head and before you know it you're really upset and even angry about it. You may want to confront your friend for being selfish and not acknowledging you when you were in a group. You may feel totally self-righteous about it too.

If you're triggered by someone else's so-called projection of you, then you need to look deeper within yourself to heal your own wounding that caused the pain or resentment in the first place.

EFT example statement for projection

Now imagine, instead of causing a big drama with your friend who really wasn't actually purposefully ignoring you, that you took 10-20 minutes for yourself to do some EFT on this trigger,

> *"Even though ... didn't acknowledge or see me, and I feel totally unseen and unheard, I unconditionally love, accept, see and acknowledge myself."*

What will happen after tapping this statement in a thorough way? You'd receive a massive inner healing on this wound, which of course relates to the mother wound of not feeling good enough. All your mental thoughts around the event will begin to calm and dissipate, as you'll find a new sense of inner freedom. You may even feel gratitude that you were able to see that it was your own projection and that your friend had brought you an immense opportunity for healing.

On the other hand, someone may genuinely cut you off mid-sentence and subtly or not so subtly put you down in front of another. In this case, you'll be called to confront the person if not straightaway, then as soon as you're able to do so. Sometimes we feel shock or taken aback when something like this happens and so can freeze and not respond immediately. I would still advise to confront the person, even if only in an email conversation. If the person refuses to look at their own behaviour and tells you that you're projecting you can explain to them their behaviour and how it made you feel. What they choose to do with this information is up to them. Your job will be done once you've expressed your truth and feelings on it. You can then also look deeper within yourself and see how this situation made you feel and tap on it. You may have felt some shock, and perhaps it also did play into a wound where you felt small or victimised. The confrontation will bring you an opportunity here to step deeper into your truth and your power by looking at your own response and taking responsibility for it by investigating and working through it step by step.

A note on Comparison and Jealousy

When we are comparing ourselves to others it is usually a sign that we need to grieve our unexpressed gifts and power. If we haven't expressed our unique gifts and talents yet there will be a longing in the heart/soul to do so, and then when we see others fulfilling their dreams it may bring up a feeling of unworthiness, pain, jealousy and comparison. Predominantly this is dealing with the mother wound of not feeling good enough and part of healing this wound is grieving our losses, that which we were never able to express due to our own disempowerment or shutdown. Once we've thoroughly grieved our unexpressed talents and power, we'll be able to step into our talents and power in a new and exciting way.

When we are comparing ourselves to others it is usually a sign that we need to grieve our unexpressed gifts and power.

47

PRACTICING CLEAR COMMUNICATION (AND HOW TO PREVENT BUILDING RESENTMENTS)

Communicating clearly

I love the simplicity of Non-Violent Communication. NVC is a simple communication process developed by Marshall Rosenberg during the 1960's. It focuses on self-empathy, empathy and an honest expression of ones needs. I'm going to give you an example of the very basics of NVC that have totally changed my world in the most awesome way. The clearer and calmer we can be when we communicate the easier it will be to solve any disagreements or misunderstandings.

So, when you feel *triggered* (uncomfortable, confused, hurt or upset) by what someone else has done or said, and after tapping on it and if it is then still appropriate, you may want to communicate it in the following way,

> *"When you did ... that made me feel ... What I really want is .... Would you be willing to give this to me?"*

In other words, you're communicating very clearly how you feel, and you're taking responsibility for it by asking for what you want and then respectfully giving them an opportunity to either give this to you or not. Resentments usually build when we assume the other person knows what we want. But how could they possibly know if we don't ask?

Listening

When we are really able to listen to others we can use the same structure to respond.

"When I did ... did it make you feel ...? Is this what you'd like to happen? Or what is it that you need?"

Giving others our full attention and presence is a healing and gift in itself. When people do not feel heard or seen it can drive them into fits of rage and violence at its most extreme. Practicing listening to others is essential along our path of awakening.

Practicing listening to others is essential along our path of awakening.

For a very long time I was not very good at listening. Because of the incredibly low self-esteem I used to have I was obsessed, even addicted to getting people to like me. I'd constantly think of clever things to say or do to win others' approval, and I'd beat myself up for weeks and months if I felt rejected or judged. I had a nasty habit of interrupting others and talking about myself, and I carried this with me into my Kundalini cleanse. As I've written before, Kundalini won't let you get away with living out of alignment. All of a sudden, I had people confront me on this habit of interrupting and talking about myself. I felt embarrassed and deeply ashamed when I was called up on it. Partly because it was true, and partly because I knew everyone else could see it too. I had to do something about it! So I began tapping on it.

EFT example statements for not listening

"Even though I talk about myself and I interrupt others, I unconditionally love and accept myself just as I am."

"Even though I need others to approve of me all the time, I unconditionally love and accept myself just as I am."

After tapping these statements and various other daily statements around this topic, I also had to be extremely conscious within all of my conversations with others. Meditation, NVC and EFT helped me to cultivate the presence I needed to become a good listener and communicator. It took a bit of time going back and forth, but I got there in the end! The amazing thing is that all of the above gave me an amazing opportunity to heal more of my mother wounding and self-esteem wounding. As I became more and more conscious of my behaviour, especially around seeking approval, I realised that it was an addiction. I began working on it, as I would work around any addiction that needed feeding, and I knew it would go as soon as I was able to approve of myself on all levels, mistakes, shadow, warts and all! And I did get there in the end.

In the beginning stages of learning how to communicate your needs and your truth I would advise to do EFT on your own or with a practitioner to strengthen your courage and also to clear out any emotional charge you may be feeling before communicating. Tapping before sending an email can be hugely helpful for this process.

When you write, instead of writing or saying, *"You did"*, or *"you are"*, you can say or write, *"I feel"* or *"that made me feel"*. Express your needs with compassion and care. You may feel as if you're dealing with the enemy, but on a greater level you're really just dealing with an aspect of yourself. How would you want to be treated in your wound by another? Compassion towards others seems to be an emotion that is cultivated as we learn to love and accept ourselves in deeper ways. As we learn to forgive ourselves it will become easier and easier to forgive others.

*Compassion towards others seems to be
an emotion that is cultivated as we learn to love
and accept ourselves in deeper ways.*

Make no assumptions

We never really know what is going on in someone else's head. Sometimes we can guess it a little bit right but often we are totally off the mark, projecting how we've been treated in the past, or how we treat others, onto the person. It really is best to avoid making any assumptions at all and to rather ask the person if you feel confused about something.

I hear too often how people assume things about others, forming judgements based on their assumptions and justifying these as if they're the absolute truth. This type of behaviour creates division and often for very little reason at all.

Be direct

No one likes to be spoken of in a negative way behind their back. Practice the golden rule, 'do onto others as you would want them to do to you'. Gossip is toxic, spreading dark seeds of judgements. It is mean and can cause a bullying gang-like reaction. Remember thoughts and words are incredibly powerful, so someone's negative words about someone else can cause them serious harm. Gossiping is also a form of psychic attack!

*Practice the golden rule, 'do onto others as you
would want them to do to you'. Gossip is toxic,
spreading dark seeds of judgements.*

Part V

CLEARING OUT AND PURIFYING YOUR SPIRITUAL BODY

What I refer to here when I write of the spiritual body or subtle energy bodies, are the bodies of energy surrounding and also entwining within and around the physical body. It is the aura and also energetic bodies of energy overlaying the physical body. It can also be referred to as the Astral, Causal, Celestial or Spiritual bodies, and all of these bodies are unique in their own way, and yet work together with the physical body in unison in order for us to be fully human.

In this section of the book I will explain to you how to neutralise and clear your energetic spiritual bodies from entities, lost deceased souls, implants or other astral attachments.

48

CLEARING THE SPIRITUAL BODY OR SUBTLE ENERGY BODIES

Energetic or astral parasites, deceased souls, entities and implants and how to neutralise these

Most people have energetic or astral attachments. It is totally normal and part of our existence and lives here on Earth. Most people can't see or feel that this is happening, but that doesn't mean it isn't happening.

If you find yourself feeling more tired, having dark thoughts, nightmares, static or crawling sensations over your physical body, especially around the ears, ringing in the ears or white noise, feeling tired, nausea or being woken up in the night in fear, then you may have an entity or astral attachment that is feeding off your energy. A deceased soul attachment is often felt in the solar plexus, and will also feel incredibly draining and tiring to the physical body. If you suspect that you have an attachment then the first and most important thing to remember is to not go into fear or panic. Ask your Higher Self to show you what it is feeding off so that you can heal authentically from the ground up, and so that nothing else could latch on once it goes. Do not talk to the being or artificial structure. It is a parasite, and it is doing what it is doing to survive and stay alive. It really isn't personal at all, so no point in getting angry or upset either.

So how do we clear negative attachments?

Take care of your basic needs. Get grounded by walking outside with your bare feet on the earth or grass. Visualising red roots or corkscrews pulling you into the earth may help to ground you, while eating root vegetable, sleep and physical exercise like dancing is incredibly grounding too.

Detoxing your physical, mental, emotional and spiritual bodies as described in this book will help you to authentically clear out old traumas and fears that may be the food these attachments are feeding off.

Stepping deeply into your power by strengthening yourself on all levels will keep entities out. Forgiveness work, which is of course incredibly empowering, is essential to keep energetic parasites at bay. Your boundaries and self-esteem need to be very clear and strong to ward off negative attachments.

Meditate to purify your mental body. Don't be afraid of meditating for long hours as a tool to purify your mental and spiritual bodies. Most mind-controlling parasites effect the mental body via the spiritual bodies.

Prayer. Commanding rather than demanding unconditional love to assist the attachment to the light. Your prayer may be answered by guiding you to a specific healing modality or healer who may then be able to assist you in removing the obstruction. Or, you may be shown what needs healing, and it may be removed from you during your dreamtime. A good healing practitioner will help you clear the wounding before assisting you in removal of the attachment.

Ask yourself how it serves you to have the attachment? Give yourself the lesson so that the attachment can drop off naturally.

Focus your energy on solutions rather than the problem.

Use healing modalities like EFT to clear out the wounding or limiting beliefs and fears that may be holding the entity in place.

Sing, even if only in the shower. Raising your voice and singing raises your vibration almost immediately!

Dancing and movement will also help you to move or shift stagnant energy.

Keep the faith!

Get your thinking out of victim consciousness and take responsibility for your life.

Be grateful for all the good in your life.

Breathwork can shift out attachments in quite a powerful way. I've seen it during workshops and experienced it in myself. The breath knows where to go, and you can just surrender and trust into the practice of the breath. Work with an experienced breath practitioner who you can be honest with regarding the attachment. It is important for you to be able to feel safe, so that you can totally let go. I recommend rebirthing and transformational breath for this.

Clear your body from Candida, heavy metal and parasitic toxicity!

Salt baths may help the process of energetic purification, but won't remove attachments unless you've healed the wound the energetic parasite is feeding off.

Clear, cancel and delete all unconscious contracts you've made with the deceased soul or fourth dimensional or astral beings concerning attachments. Clear all contracts to assist other beings to the light, etc. Speak these out loud in a powerful assertive voice.

These energetic parasites ALWAYS bring us an opportunity to step deeper into our spiritual empowerment and purity.

The first time I physically felt an attachment I went into a state of panic and fear. I was judged by those around me at the time, as I also judged myself. I really had no understanding of what was happening to me, and so I had to learn the slow and hard way. One important thing to remember is that your Higher Self will always be present during this process, assisting your soul back to wholeness and radical freedom. You are not forgotten or alone. If you can feel attachments it means you're sensitively tuned in, and that your vibration is probably quite high. Think of it, as you would think of head lice or other bodily parasites, like worms. It is purely an astral parasitic manifestation and by-product of our unconscious shadow and fears.

These energetic parasites ALWAYS bring us an opportunity to step deeper into our spiritual empowerment and purity.

A Prayer for Clearing of Unconscious Contracts and Vows

"Mother Father Divine within, Unconditional Love, I Am Presence,

Thank you for clearing out, deleting and cancelling any contracts or vows that I have made consciously or unconsciously on all levels and dimensions of my being over all time and space where I have agreed for this being or attachment to disempower or feed off my energy. I now claim back my body, mind and soul and command single soul occupancy within my physical vessel. I now step deeply into my power and am grateful to be shown any wounding that needs to heal, for my being in order to be radically free. I know that this will be shown to me with ease and grace, and in the highest and best way for my soul's evolution. I now free myself from all negative contracts and vows on all levels of my being. I am sovereign and I am free.

It is done, and so it is. Aho/Amen/Thank You."

Figure 13: How to Clear Negative Attachments

- Take care of your basic needs. Get grounded
- Detox your physical, mental, emotional & spiritual bodies
- Step deeply into your power
- Meditate
- Use Prayer
- Ask yourself firmly how it serves you to have the attachment
- Focus your energy on solutions
- Use healing modalities like EFT for clearing
- Sing, even if only in the shower!
- Dance, exercise and movement
- Keep the Faith!
- Move out of victim consciousness - take responsibility for your life
- Be grateful for all the good in your life
- The power of Breathwork
- Clear your body from Candida, heavy metals & parasitic toxicity
- Take salt baths
- Clear, cancel and delete all unconscious contracts

49

FALSE LIGHT VERSUS UNCONDITIONAL LOVE

"The pure and perfect humans who act like perpetual gods or goddesses come to coerce, control and imprison us. The ones who will help us to heal and set us free come wandering through the bone yard, crawling from the swamp, covered in filth, imperfect, dancing and grieving." Jason Hine[3]

There is what I refer to as false light energy which is a fake light that covers up the darkness, the unconscious and our shadow. This false light works hand in hand with the more obvious dark unconscious energy as opposite sides to the same coin, and then there is unconditional, conscious, fierce, powerful love. *False light* plays itself off against the dark, but subtly or not so subtly, allows the dark or unconscious energy to prevail, whereas *unconditional love* is strong and boundaried when needed and powerful beyond measure. False light wants people to be confused, disempowered, victimised and energetically open with no boundaries. It wants you giving your power away to governments, mainstream medicine, and false light beings rather than empowering yourself by taking responsibility for yourself and going ever inwards as you become more and more self-realised and spiritually empowered.

You do not need to be saved by anything outside of yourself in

3 Hine, J (2018) Personal Communication (Facebook, **date**)

order to be free. People are told and sold to do certain things in order to receive eternal salvation, and they are threatened with eternal damnation and Hell if they don't! Little do they know that eternal salvation can only be found when we actually do the inner necessary work required for our souls to be radically free. We can spiritually bypass, stay in victim consciousness, or go into denial for many lifetimes, but eventually the soul, that always wants to be authentically free, will make a course correction to find its way back to its purity and authentic powerful expression again.

> *Eternal salvation can only be found when we actually do the inner necessary work required for our souls to be radically free.*

Astral or 4th dimensional false light beings may present themselves to you and ask you to channel, or to perform so-called 'good deeds', and you may feel special (this energy playing into your ego/low self-esteem wounding), that you have been chosen to do this 'good work', but if it is false light, it will usually be exhausting and distracting you from your soul's work to awaken from the ground up by purifying your physical, mental, emotional and spiritual bodies until you are authentically and radically free.

For this very reason, I am highly suspicious of channelled messages and channelling in general. Often 98 percent of the information will be spot on and even helpful, and then there will be two or five percent misinformation thrown in there to keep the students or listeners disempowered and in check, coming back for more, and unable to trust their own hearts. Why can't these beings be born into this world? Why do they need to take over someone's physical body? It just doesn't make much sense to me. Often channelled messages will sound a bit like this, "*We come to you from the stars, and we see your concern for the planet. We are here to bring you the divine message that your suffering will soon come to an end*". These messages will keep you in an energy of hope for the future, looking ever forward, hoping for collective salvation and keeping you in disempowerment. Forget these messages! Go inwards, get grounded and get real! All these messages are doing is causing good-hearted people to get distracted from their inner purification and spiritual empowerment process.

False light wants to pull you out of your physical body, leaving you weak and fragile, disempowered and open to the unconscious, the dark, or astral attachments, whereas the true authentic awakening energy of unconditional love will ground you inwards pulling you down into your body so that you can be in your core strength, power and stability awakening from the base or ground up.

There are many false light gurus, shamans, preachers, spiritual teachers, etc. who subtly or not so subtly feed off the energy they receive from their disciples and/or clients/followers. I cannot stress enough how important it is to not give your power away to others. You know you're giving your power away when you're in awe of others, placing them on a spiritual pedestal. It is true that some people are further spiritually evolved than others, but this does not make them any more special! We all have the same value! A true authentic spiritual teacher, shaman or healer will point you to yourself, assisting you in empowering yourself as you heal and unfold along your unique soul's evolution.

> *It is true that some people are further spiritually evolved than others, but this does not make them any more special!*

Be aware of spiritual teachers and shamans who have distorted sexual energy and due to a lack of enough inner awareness are still acting out of their own sexual wounding. I've helped many clients who've been negatively affected and even traumatised by this type of manipulative energy. Guard your body and your spirit with care, self-love and respect.

True unconditional love is unafraid to be fierce and even righteously angry if need be. Love is not only birdsong and rainbows, but it is also a fierce storm or a lion's roar!

If your child is verbally attacked by someone in front of you, you won't just stand there saying, *"it is all perfect"*, *"I'm going to be neutral"*, or *"we must be good and forgive"*. No, you will step in and say no to the perpetrator. Fierce unconditional love is a firm boundary to unconscious false light and more obviously dark energies. Righteous anger and firm boundaries does not make you a bad or fearful person! When we're disempowered we'll stay in confusion, making excuses for the bullies, swallowing down our truths, etc. When we're spiritual empowered we'll stand up for ourselves and others when being wrongfully attacked or harmed.

> *True unconditional love is unafraid to be fierce and even angry if need be. Love is not only birdsong and rainbows, but it is also a fierce storm or a lion's roar!*

We need to become totally ok and even at peace with being wrongfully accused, judged and disliked by others. People don't always want to be pulled up on their unconscious behaviour and may attack, hate, judge, reject, etc. No one ever said that this journey of personal spiritual empowerment and radical freedom would be easy. We need to be very brave to embark on this soul purification journey, as we may eventually lose every single person in our lives as we change and grow. Imagine having to face every single unconscious fear you have in order to free yourself? Being free is awesome and totally worth the inner work, but the journey from disempowerment to empowerment can be very challenging. We cannot bypass integrating and healing our shadow and fears along our journey towards radical freedom.

Don't be fooled by the 'nice' masks people wear to manipulate and control. It is false light that teaches our children to always be good, nice and sweet, even at the expense of their own truth, power and boundaries. We are taught that we're bad or wrong when our actions upset others, and so we begin to swallow down our truth and power allowing for others to manipulate and control us. This is how the paedophile will find his/her victim, or the psychopath her/his enabler. When we shut ourselves and our truth down due to false light fears of upsetting others we begin to coerce with the dark! This

236

entire journey from unconsciousness to consciousness is about your power and energy. Your energy can either feed the dark and false light, or you can keep your energy for YOU and become spiritually full of your own energy. When you're full of your own energy you will feel really strong and aligned. You'll be able to give more to others, not from a place of leaking energy or obligation and guilt, but rather from a place of abundance and empowerment assisting others in empowering themselves too.

50

THE FALSE REALITY
MATRIX CONSTRUCT

"What is it, don Juan?" I asked.

"Long ago, the native sorcerer/shamans of Mexico discovered that we have a companion for life," he said, as clearly as he could.

"We have a predator that came from the depths of the cosmos, and took over the rule of our lives. Human beings are its prisoners. The predator is our lord and master. It has rendered us docile; helpless. If we want to protest, it suppresses our protest. If we want to act independently, it demands that we don't do so."

"Why has this predator taken over in the fashion that you're describing, don Juan?" I asked. "There must be a logical explanation."

"There is an explanation," don Juan replied, "which is the simplest explanation in the world. They took over because we are food for them, and they squeeze us mercilessly because we are their sustenance. Just as we rear chickens in chicken coops, gallineros, the predators rear us in human coops, humaneros. Therefore, their food is always available to them."

"In order to keep us obedient, meek and weak, the predators engaged themselves in a stupendous manoeuvre — stupendous, of course, from the point of view of a fighting strategist; a horrendous manoeuvre from the point of view of those who suffer it. They gave us their mind! Do you hear me? The predators give us their mind which becomes our mind. The predators' mind is baroque, contradictory, morose, and filled with the fear of being discovered any minute now."

"But why is it that the sorcerers of ancient Mexico and all sorcerers today, although they see the predators, don't do anything about it?"

"There's nothing that you and I can do about it," don Juan said in a grave, sad voice. "All we can do is discipline ourselves to the point where they will not touch us."

Carlos Castaneda[4]

We are all born into a world where we are taught to suppress our feelings in order to be accepted, where the air we breathe, the food we eat, and the water we drink is toxic. We are losing massive chunks of our rainforests yearly and we poison our oceans with dirty oil and rubbish. TV, media, most mainstream films, drugs and pornography tend to dumb humans down keeping them distracted, in fear and disempowerment. People are told that they're free to vote, to make a change, but in reality, we are enslaved to corrupt political and monetary systems. Do not be fooled. You are not free until you've freed yourself on ALL levels of your being.

After my Kundalini awakening in 2013 I was shown the truth of humanity's enslavement by a fourth dimensional parasitic extra-terrestrial race, and was horrified by what I saw. It took me around six months to come to terms with this information. I just couldn't wrap my head around this new way of seeing or experiencing reality. My entire life I had felt safely cocooned in the false matrix reality system of distractions and disempowerment. Now, after purifying

---

4   Castenada, C (1998) *The Active Side of Inifinity*, Harper Collins, New York

for around 15 years quite extensively, I was shown a deeper level of truth, and that humans were not at the top of the food chain! But by seeing and knowing this truth in my being I was given an opportunity to step deeper into my own spiritual empowerment and freedom. You see, before my awakening I truly believed that if I just focussed my thoughts on good things that I would attract only good things. I believed I was safe, loved and free, and that I had many angels and spiritual guides around me. So, when I was shown the truth of these astral parasites, and the depth of this conspiracy, how it affected every single human being on this planet, I was totally shocked and horrified. I was living in 'spiritual' La La land, and then awoke to a very sinister truth, almost exactly as it is portrayed in the film "The Matrix".

Since my awakening I have discovered that there are many healers and awakened individuals that are aware of this truth. In other words, it's not only me who woke up to this truth! Jesus in the Christian Bible referred to these beings as *demons*; the Gnostics, in the Gnostic gospels referred to these beings as the *archons*; the shaman Don Juan, whom Carlos Castaneda worked with, referred to these beings as *predators* and/or *flyers* as seen in the exert above; and in Islam they refer to these beings as the *Djin*. It is not a new story, but a very old one.

The sad truth is that most people do not yet want to be disturbed from watching 'The X-Factor', eating at McDonalds, taking drugs, or working their way up the corporate ladder. It serves these negative astral beings well for humanity to look the other way too. In many ways, this dark consciousness has become a part of us, as they've been parasitising off our consciousness for eons. They have highly sophisticated technologies to keep us enslaved and mind controlled. There are some people who argue that we have been genetically engineered specifically for this purpose.

It is very important not to get panicked or fearful regarding this information though. Either we go into fear, drama and panic, which is what I did initially, and it definitely made things worse for me. Or we can focus on the solution, the beautiful pearl that is being shaped by the parasite. As we begin to focus on healing ourselves from the ground up, clearing out toxins from our physical bodies, stuck emotions and trauma, while practicing powerful spiritual mental body clearing tools such as meditation and EFT, these beings and their devices will authentically drop off, never to return.

I was guided to forgive the play of duality on this planet. Acceptance is another word for forgiveness, but that doesn't mean I condone the dark. It means I have faith in the process of my awakening at a very deep level. I've also been shown to focus my energy on solutions and gratitude rather than the problems, again not to deny, but not to get sucked into fear, and to rather bring in the light of fierce unconditional love, empowerment, boundaries, faith and trust which is the only true way to overcome this unconscious dark energy!

It benefits us to focus our attention on UNCONDITIONAL LOVE and spiritual empowerment that is beyond duality.

Remember that false light and unconscious energy keeps us in the battle, the struggle, disempowered and victimised. It benefits us to focus our attention on UNCONDITIONAL LOVE and spiritual empowerment that is beyond duality. Once we are able to forgive even these dark entities and their sinister control systems, we will be shown how we can be part of the solution. And remember that forgiving this consciousness doesn't mean we are condoning it! But it is no good fighting this negative unconscious energy when we're disempowered and victimised, as we're fighting from a place of fear and unconsciousness, and two wrongs never make a right. When we're fully empowered, conscious and free then unconscious energy can't touch us, and we're then able to shine the light for others to free themselves too. When enough of us free ourselves authentically then this dark controlling system will have to collapse. When there is no more food for these beings to feed off, the game is over.

So truly the only way to solve this problem is to begin the process of purifying all of your bodies, integrating your shadow, busting through your fears, and staying grounded in faith and trust as you work your way to radical freedom and soul sovereignty. It is truly our choice whether we want to be a part of the problem or part of the solution.

There are also 5th Dimensional beings, like angels and spirits guides who are working alongside us to assist us in our awakening. We aren't totally alone against these negative astral beings, but can also call on our spirit guides, our angels, animal guides and those beings who love us unconditionally to support us through our awakening process. It isn't disempowering to allow for a truly loving guide to guide us out of a challenging situation. These guides or angels will always work in such a way to empower us, so that we're able to learn and grow deeply from the inside out.

EFT example statements for astral attachments

> *"Even though I have an attachment, I unconditionally love and accept myself exactly as I am, and I trust that I am exactly where I am meant to be on my path of awakening."*

> *"Even though I feel stuck and unable to break free from my dark thoughts, I unconditionally love and accept myself as I step into my spiritual power."*

> *"Even though I feel like a victim of these attachments/darkness, I now take full responsibility for my life and am grateful that I am learning to step deeply into my soul's empowerment and freedom."*

It is truly our choice whether we want to be a part of the problem or the solution.

A Prayer for Astral Attachments

"Mother Father Divine within, Unconditional Love, I Am Presence,

Thank you for strengthening my faith as I step deeper into myself and my spiritual empowerment. I trust that I am exactly where I am meant to be, and I am grateful for learning what my soul is needing to learn in order to be free. Thank you for assisting me on my path to radical freedom.

It is done, and so it is. Aho/Amen/Thank You."

EPILOGUE

"Don't ask what the world needs. Ask what makes you come alive, and go do it. Because what the world needs are people who have come alive."

Howard Thurman

We may of course at times be called to step into our warrior selves and to fight our own unique fight in our own unique way. Standing firm in the power of fierce unconditional love doesn't mean we become complacent in the face of darkness or false light. There will be times when we'll need to step into our courage, stand up or express our truth, say no, and even go into battle, whether that battle is metaphorical or not. The more we can allow for ourselves to shift with ease from our warrior selves into our softer expressions and back again if needed, the more we'll be in the natural flow of our authentic expression. It is about allowing ourselves to embody all of our varied expressions without staying stuck in a particular way for too long.

We are all dancing our unique individual dances, and sometimes our expression is inwards and still, while other times we may find ourselves shining outwards connecting fully with everyone around us. Allowing for balance between our internal sun and moon, masculine and feminine energies are of course essential along our path of awakening.

Honouring our sacred internal rhythms means we'll have the energy to give when needed, as long as it is balanced with receiving. Allowing ourselves to receive without guilt or shame is an expression of self-love and kindness. It may take time and practice to get it right, to really open our hearts wide as we receive so that we can fully let it all in, and why not? We deserve to receive joy, love, gratitude, kindness, support and goodness into our lives. When our inner cup is overflowing we are easily able to give to others.

Be brave and let go of relationships that are holding you back from being your true authentic self. You know the ones I'm referring to here, where you're walking on eggshells, or where the energy is sickly nice keeping you attached in an energy of obligation or manipulation. Love yourself enough to stand alone for a while if you must. Keep looking ever inwards in silence, meditation, presence and self-observation and admit when you've made a mistake so that you can learn what you need to learn in order to truly free yourself and move forward.

We deserve to receive joy, love, gratitude, kindness, support and goodness into our lives. When our inner cup is overflowing we are easily able to give to others.

I made a decision to wake up this lifetime and my Higher Self has been working what feels like overtime to assist me in this process. It IS possible, and the cycles of healing our past wounding will eventually evaporate into thin air as we set ourselves free to this present moment. Everything here on earth, our relationships, our work, our hobbies and gifts, are all here for us to grow and expand, so that we can spiritually evolve and be free to flow in synchronicity while creating our dreams into reality.

Within every new life cycle, whether it be a project, a relationship or your spiritual awakening, the beginning is always a time when you'll feel vulnerable or a little uneasy on your feet. Trust that you are held safely in life and the Divine's loving embrace. Life is an incredible experience, and within it lies an immense opportunity for us to turn our base metal and pain into our soul's golden authentic expression. We must be willing to feel it all, our pain, our joy, our rage, our fierce compassion and love, our grief and passion. To fully feel everything is to be alive and here in the not knowing, the messy and unpredictable now. Many times over I've had clients on my couch still pushing their feelings down with shame. Oh, the sweet relief after an outburst of rage or a decent out-loud sob!

As you begin to raise your energetic frequency by purifying all of your bodies, you'll also be assisting in the awakening of the collective on this planet. We are at the brink of an incredible collective awakening, but to really assist in this collective awakening we must be willing to dive deeply inwards into our shadowy darkness to find our authentic light. You are the being appointed for this soul satisfying and empowering inner work. Don't allow yourself to get distracted by the false reality matrix construct. You will be tested along the way many times over, even go through the 'black night of the soul', and you will rise each and every time triumphing over these obstacles, as long as you are willing to do the necessary inner work to free yourself fully. It is not an overnight process! It will take time and determination, but if you decide to awaken, your Higher Self will begin the process of soul purification on all levels as you follow the signs and synchronicities along the way. You will get lost, in a muddle and confused at times, but you will be guided back on your soul's path as long as you keep that candle of faith burning in your heart, letting go of control and perfectionism, and surrendering into inner trust.

We are at the brink of an incredible collective awakening, but to really assist in this collective awakening we must be willing to dive deeply inwards into our shadowy darkness to find our authentic light.

It is not an easy journey, as life can be filled with loss and pain. It is easy to go into autopilot, numbing out with addictive behaviours, not wanting to feel, but the price we pay for this is the death of our soul's authentic expression and aliveness. If we want to be truly ALIVE we must allow for our emotions to flow while listening to our feelings, as we express ourselves in our unique authentic ways.

"You have brains in your head
You have feet in your shoes.
You can steer yourself in any direction you choose"
Dr Seuss, 'Oh, The Places You'll Go'

So, get started, and make the most of your unique life journey. Turn your life into a great adventure! From caterpillar to gloriously winged butterfly, as you learn, evolve and grow, know that you are ultimately setting yourself radically free to allow for the Divine to shine through YOU in your own unique way. No one else can do this for you. Only you can be the one to free you!

Everything in this book is to help you along your journey to radical freedom. And remember you have LIFE teaching you, communicating with you, holding you, and sometimes allowing for you to go through pain and darkness to find your inner strength, love and soul light. Trust in yourself. Trust in LIFE. Trust in the Divine. Laugh at your demons. Go with the flow and NEVER ever give your power away to anyone else. Honour the divine feminine and masculine within yourself and others. Heal your mother and father wounding with patience, self-acceptance and love. Focus your energy on solutions! Put time and effort into your dreams, your gifts and talents, and shine your soul light shamelessly like the sun.

Awakening to your authentic true human self has
nothing to do with 'being spiritual'. We cannot
become or be spiritual, as we already are spiritual.
Awakening is in its essence about becoming a fully
integrated and grounded human being.

A Prayer for Humanity

"Mother Father Divine within, Unconditional Love, I Am Presence,

Thank you for assisting humanity in our awakening to the truth and power of who we really are, so that we can take responsibility and make the necessary changes that need to be made for a new and peaceful world. May all beings be sovereign, free, grounded and authentically happy.

It is done, and so it is. Aho/Amen/Thank You."

Final note

Awakening to your authentic true human self has nothing to do with 'being spiritual'. We cannot become or be spiritual, as we already are spiritual. Awakening is in its essence about becoming a fully integrated and grounded human being. If for any reason you are feeling overwhelmed with all of the changes that you know you need to make in order to free yourself authentically just come back into yourself, in this moment and know that you are exactly where you are meant to be. And if you're finding this difficult then tap it into your consciousness. Remember that it takes time and patience as we heal the layers and layers of trauma, shame and fear. As long as you keep going inwards to feel what is there in order to release the past, and as long as you are expressing your truth, stepping into more and more of who you really are beyond all conditioning, you're well on your awakening journey. And even though we are moving towards a new and brighter way of being and living it all starts exactly where you are. And if all feels lost and broken beyond repair this is your opportunity to build on new and solid ground. Focus on solutions and find the courage to birth yourself like a phoenix rising from the ashes into a bright new form.

ABOUT THE AUTHOR

Louisa Love is a trained T.A.S.K Kinesiologist, author and facilitator who specialises in kinesiology and also works with healing techniques like Emotional Freedom Technique, Emotional Stress Release, Matrix Reimprinting, Australian Bush Flower Remedies, Meditation and also intuitively with Breathwork. She also works with herbs and nutrition and specialises in healing the gut and emotions. Experiencing a dramatic and ungrounded Kundalini Awakening in 2013 and working with the guidance of her Higher Self and life to heal in an even deeper and more authentic way, she now assists her clients to awaken safely from the ground up. Louisa works one-to-one in private sessions and is also available for Skype sessions, workshops and also group retreats.

For more information on sessions, workshops and retreats go to www.louisahealing.com

LOUISA LOVE

Find *How to be Radically Free* on Facebook

What people are saying about Louisa's work and *How to be Radically Free*:

"Louisa has to my mind the most incredible healing skills that I have ever encountered. I am lucky enough to have met, interviewed and worked with many healers. There is something about Louisa's approach and healing skills that is out of the ordinary and totally special. I have recommended Louisa to many friends who have all been left feeling about her work as I do – that she has a unique and very specially highly tuned ability to heal. Expect miracles!"

Dana Amma Day (*Positive News*)

"I could easily throw out all of my self-help books and only refer to this one. How to be Radically Free *is definitely my Desert Island book."*

Jenny E, Seeker of Truth

NOTES

NOTES

Proof

Made in the USA
Columbia, SC
23 July 2018